Hertfordshire
COUNTY COUNCIL
Community Information

11 JAN 2003

2|12

Please renew/return this item by the last date shown.

So that your telephone call is charged at local rate,
please call the numbers as set out below:

	From Area codes 01923 or 0208:	From the rest of Herts:
Renewals:	01923 471373	01438 737373
Enquiries:	01923 471333	01438 737333
Minicom:	01923 471599	01438 737599

L32

D1349609

GREATER LOVE

Letters Home 1914–1918

GREATER LOVE

Letters Home 1914–1918

edited by

Michael Moynihan

W. H. ALLEN · LONDON
A Howard & Wyndham Company
1980

Photoset, printed and bound in Great Britain by
REDWOOD BURN LIMITED
Trowbridge & Esher
for the publishers, W.H. Allen & Co. Ltd.,
44 Hill Street, London W1X 8LB

ISBN 0 491 02830 X

Acknowledgements

I am greatly indebted to the Imperial War Museum for access to their archives. In particular I would like to thank Mr Roderick Suddaby, Head of the Department of Documents, for his expert assistance in selecting material, and to the Reading Room staff for help with research.

I am much obliged for the valuable background information supplied by Mr Robert McGregor, Mrs Katharine Cleasby-Thompson, Mrs Ivy Sweeney, Mrs Doris Finch, Mr William Ward-Jackson, Captain Eric Bush, Mrs Audrey Robinson and Mrs Louise Downer.

Finally I owe a debt of gratitude to the Editor of *The Sunday Times*, Mr Harold Evans, without whose support and encouragement work on this book would not have been possible. Grateful thanks are also due to Mr Magnus Linklater, Assistant Editor.

Contents

Preface

The Great War was a time when the bromide flourished. Every Tommy blown to pieces or gassed or caught by a stray bullet died a hero's death for King and Country. In pulpits, in letters of condolence, later on war memorials, one bromide excelled all others: Greater love hath no man than this, that a man lay down his life for his friends.

Among the letters that follow there is evidence enough that the trenches bred a spirit of self-sacrifice and camaraderie rarely encountered in peacetime. But that is not the primary theme of this book. The love here reflected is the common currency of love: but a love intensified, refined, made more precious, with death so close.

The six writers of these letters have very different backgrounds: a middle-aged Scottish musician, a young Sandhurst-trained officer, a Cockney Tommy, a 'brass hat' from the landed gentry, a boy midshipman, and a Sussex schoolmaster and father of thirteen. But whether it is to wife, sweetheart, parents or son that they write, the loving motivation of their letters is the same. Five of them were on active service, on the Western Front and at Gallipoli. Two were killed in action.

This is the sixth book I have edited from the diaries, letters and journals of ordinary participants in the two world wars. All of them have come to light in recent years, either acquired by the Department of Documents of the Imperial War Museum or submitted by readers of *The Sunday Times*. In many cases they have been found gathering dust in an attic or at the back of a drawer after the death of the veteran author or his widow. They are much rarer than may be supposed.

Having in mind the millions of letters that flooded from the various theatres of war between 1914 and 1918, it is tragic to consider how many of equal quality to these must have been consigned to the dustbin as of no further interest or value. For letters have a unique power of evoking history in the making. Unlike diaries, which are essentially self-conscious exercises, or journals, written in retrospect and with publication in mind, letters can be trusted to describe things as they really were, at a given time, in a given place, and to reveal a man as he was seen by those closest to him, warts and all.

One might imagine that there was nothing new left to be said about the Great War. Yet there are revelations in some of these letters that come with a shock of surprise. How many are aware, for example, that during every major battle in Flanders and Picardy the sound of the guns could be clearly and persistently heard in southern England ('like the thud of some giant propeller' as schoolmaster Robert Saunders put it)? Or that, from the outbreak of the war, hundreds of boys of school age served aboard warships, sometimes in the thick of action? Or that a divisional headquarters close to the front line could be so out of touch with what was going on that, at the end of the first day of the Battle of the Somme, a day on which 19,240 British officers and men had been killed and tens of thousands more wounded, a staff officer could blithely write that 'our casualties have not been very heavy'?

But it is as human documents, rather than footnotes to history, that these letters make their strongest appeal. 'I seem to love you deeper and better than I have ever done,' writes Private Peter McGregor to his adored wife on the eve of his departure to the trenches from which he will not return. 'Oh! you simply have been haunting me lately,' writes Captain Douglas Talbot amid the carnage of Gallipoli to the girl he has left behind (and who will treasure his love all her life). Love stories with unhappy endings – but in reading them it is the heightened awareness of the joys of life that lingers, and death seems robbed of its sting.

Most war letters that have been deemed worthy of preservation were written by men at the front. A particular rarity are the letters in the final chapter from a father to his son, which give a vivid impression of life on the home front. What may be usefully repeated here is the indication they give of the gulf that existed between combatant and civilian throughout the war. Far more than in the Second World War, when the serviceman overseas had as much cause for anxiety about his loved ones at home as they for him, soldiers on leave from the trenches felt themselves in an alien world. Hysteria over air-raids (in which 1413 were killed, compared with 60,595 in the Second World War), grumbles over food shortages and high prices and restrictions generally, seemed out of all proportion to their own ordeals. Patriotic jingoism struck a false note. Hatred for the Hun did not tally with their feelings for 'Jerry', enduring the same conditions of shellfire, mud, rats and lice in their trenches the other side of no-man's land.

That men at the front could be surprisingly unreticent in attempting to convey horrific experiences is shown by some of these letters. But such intimations of the dehumanised, degrading business trench warfare had become were too much at variance with what one read in the papers or heard from propaganda platforms and pulpits to sink in. 'As one's experience of "hell" is limited,' Robert Saunders observed, 'it is rather difficult to get a picture in your mind.' And in

x

the reaction of Private McGregor's wife to one such letter one can sense how loving concern must have been intensified by that gap in understanding. 'I can't think how you've stood it so well,' she writes. 'I suppose you would shut that mouth and stick out that stubborn chin and just "stick it".'

Love, physical and platonic, marital, parental and filial, are all mirrored in the letters that follow. On a different plane are love for home and country, for comrades-in-arms and regiment. Most difficult to define is that kind of love peculiar to war, half zest for battle, half death-wish, for which 'death or glory' was the accepted bromide.

When Captain Talbot writes after the Gallipoli landings of having seen death all round him and of finding it 'very beautiful', and of tears of pride coming to his eyes at the thought of the British Tommy 'hurling himself to death with a smile on his face and a cheer on his lips', 'sick' is the word that might nowadays come to mind. But it is a sentiment not infrequently encountered in diaries, letters and forgotten poems of the Great War, particularly among young officers who might seem to have had most to live for.

'A Plea for War' was the title of one poem of a kind poles apart from the agonised and bitter poetry of Wilfred Owen and Siegfried Sassoon, but admired in its day. Published in the *Westminster Gazette*, it was written by a young Coldstream Guards officer, Denis Buxton, son of the Governor-General of South Africa and an old Etonian of brilliant promise, who was later killed in action at Ypres. A typical verse reads:

There never were such days as these to scan
  The God in man –
And praised be war, if only that it brings
  Rest from the weary strife with little things.

Such feelings are as remote from us as those of the mother of a Dartmouth cadet (quoted in Chapter 5) when she wrote that 'if my son can best serve England by giving his life for her, I would not lift one finger to bring him home', and who glorified death as 'a mighty and glorious Angel, setting on the brow the crown of immortality.'

Words such as these have a hollow ring today, but were golden currency at the time. A time when life was cheap, and love, in all its aspects, the more prized.

Chapter 1

'My Dear Darling Sweet Wife . . .'

When Private Peter McGregor of the 14th Argyll and Sutherland Highlanders was killed on the Western Front on 13 September 1916, his widow in Edinburgh was left in no doubt as to the special esteem and affection in which he had been held by his comrades.

'Universally beloved in the Battalion', 'a great favourite, one of the best known men in his Company', 'a centre of cheerfulness and good humour', were among the phrases used in five letters of condolence (from battalion commander to chaplain) that go far beyond the stock tributes of 'devotion to duty' and 'Greater love hath no man'.

But in the almost daily letters he wrote to his wife Janet during his fifteen months' army service (three of them at the front, one has to read between the lines to appreciate the personal sense of loss that was evidently felt, by officers and men alike. From his own modest accounts he emerges less as the life and soul of the party than as the odd man out: laughing at himself in his unlikely role as a Tommy, resolutely acclimatising himself during training to the swearing, boozing and licentiousness of his fellow-soldiery, frankly terrified of shellfire in the trenches, and concealing a constant homesickness behind a cheery front.

It seems likely that McGregor would have more readily recog-

1

nised himself in the modest tribute paid to him in the monthly magazine of St Andrew's Church, Edinburgh, shortly after his death: 'Peter McGregor was known to many as organist and choirmaster at St Andrew's. On our streets when he was home on leave he was always a noteable figure, never lounging or playing at his new business, but taking it in earnest like a soldier born. He would not have refused the supreme sacrifice, but many hearts are sore for his wife and young children.'

Among the collections of letters from the First World War that have come to light, McGregor's stand out for the ardency of the love they express. In numerous passages to his 'dear darling sweet wife' one might be reading the passionate endearments of a young newly-wed rather than (as transpires) a family man in his forties, with a daughter of nine and son of eight. 'Don't be down – things will come alright,' he writes shortly before embarking for the front. 'There is one thing, I seem to love you deeper and better than I have ever done.'

For Janet McGregor it must have been a painful reflection that, but for a white lie, her choirmaster husband might never have found himself in the trenches. Towards the end of his training, when she is suggesting making an application on his behalf for a commission, he writes: 'Don't for goodness sake give my birth certificate to anyone. My age in this battalion is 36, born 1879. If they knew I was older I would be put into some of the home battalions, and when all's said and done I don't want to be.'

Born in October 1871, McGregor came from a middle-class family of nine, the eldest of five brothers. His father was a professional painter, exhibiting at the Royal Scottish Academy, and it was as an art student of his that Janet Davidson first met Peter. His first surviving letter to her is an invitation to hear him play at a violin and piano recital in 1902 with his sister Helen. The programme (describing them as 'two members of the well-known artiste family') introduces Peter as a pupil of 'the greatest teacher of the piano in the world, Professor Theodor

2

Leschetizky of Vienna', and eulogises his expressive playing and 'great poetical feeling'.

He appears to have had no very high opinion of himself, however. In a letter from Vienna to a sister in 1899, on his twenty-eighth birthday, he writes: 'I am getting beastly old and not done anything. . . . By nature I am a recluse – I am awfully afraid to do anything and keep very quiet, dream away and wish.' Even sixteen years later, during the early part of his training in 1915, he describes himself in a letter to his wife as 'the quiet Pete, who liked more than anything to be quiet, lazy perhaps – to love his wife and play Debussy – try and paint – draw and read – and dream the days away.'

That such a man not only survived the gruelling square-bashing, route marches and field-days with men half his age but grew to relish much of it, and that he later took on his jutting chin the horrors of trench warfare, indicates depths of character which would have remained hidden had he sheltered behind his birth certificate. Eight months after enlisting he writes: 'I am beginning to live now – life has a different view to me – my eyes are, I am sure, wider open than they have ever been.'

A patriot and proud of his clan ancestry, McGregor had had some training with a group of local volunteers before enlisting. And a letter to his wife (away on a visit) in April 1915 makes it clear that he had weighed the consequences. 'I was glad to hear that Robin was so sure that every man would be needed. I am quite ready. I have no doubt you will be a widow yet – fascinating one too, and would like to marry you myself again if I could come back – ah well you would have peace, no husband to bother you – Oh I would be sorry to leave you – fancy never coming back – only a memory – however I am ready to go. I have learned enough of drill and can shoot fairly well and have no doubt would give a good account of myself in the field of battle. . . .'

McGregor's letters to his 'darling Jen', mostly written in pencil in a flowing hand, the bulk during his twelve-months' *training in Hampshire and Surrey, amount to over 500,000 words. Concentrating on his letters from the trenches, it is only possible in the confines of this chapter to give brief glimpses of the camp life and rigorous training he writes about at length, and usually with gusto.*

In this section emphasis has been given to the expressions of love that glow at the heart of almost every letter (reciprocated, if with more restraint, in the few of his wife's daily letters to him that have survived). Once at the front, with the knowledge that an officer in his battalion would be censoring everything he wrote, McGregor became seemingly shy of exposing his deepest feelings.

13 June 1915. Plymouth

My dear darling wife,

It is one of the most difficult things in the world to write – we sit about in batches, everybody is joined together by a brotherly feeling – everybody shares their things. I am sitting out on the side of a hill overlooking Plymouth. I have had a busy time drilling and eating – the food is not bad. . . .

Yesterday I was inoculated – my arm is yellow and purple and feels a bit stiff. The Doctor that inoculated me said, 'Here's a cheery chap' (I was smiling) – men were fainting and others were turning pale but I put a broad grin on and watched the needle pushed into my arm.

We were forming companies yesterday – men were fainting and turning sick. There are some windy specimens here, and some awful looking characters. There are some quite decent fellows in our hut, and some rather coarse ones. The language is sometimes lurid, in fact some of the men can't say three words without at least one of them being swear-words.

The Corporal is a boozy swearing old soldier – I would call him a blackguard. He was fearfully drunk last night and in the middle of the night he went out and got lost, the noise he made when he came in was awful. We turn in at 9.30. Lights out at 10.10. . . .

I wish you could see me in our hut – and hear the stories that are told and the awful songs that are sung. Before lights went out last night we had an impromptu sing-song. I played a solo on my pipe and I told a naughty story. We soon get to know each other and there is no ceremony – everybody talks to everybody else. . . .

The life is fine but of course it is not home – once or twice I had watery eyes thinking of my dear ones at home. On Friday afternoon we went out for a short route march – pipers – we fell in on the Barracks Square and marched down the road – a typical English lane, very beautiful. I enjoyed it very much. . . .

My bed is a thing stuffed with straw, one of my blankets I wrap round it and the other two I cover myself with. I use a pair of army socks as bed socks – keep my feet nice and warm as it is chilly in the early morning. I am becoming quite a hardened Tommy. If you could see me crowding into the mess hut for my meals – carrying my knife and fork and spoon – you would laugh – drinking tea out of a pudding bowl. It's great I tell you.

Now that you have my address you might send me some dainties – a cake, fancy biscuits, toffee, sweets occasionally – and papers, we get none here. Don't send too much as I might be considered a toff you know – just a little. . . . I forgot to bring my sketch book, the very small one lying in my music cabinet left hand side. I am going now and have a wash up and shave – in the meantime farewell.

Finished that job – I wonder if you will be able to find 'Sea Pieces' by McDowall and the 'Russian Dances' on top of the drawers. I don't know what I have said but between

5

the lines are all my thoughts of you and the dear large babies. Bob would just love to see his Dad in my straw bed and see him drill. Tell Margaret I saw a wee girl when out on the route march – and my eyes filled with tears thinking I wouldn't see my dear darling family for such a long time.

Love to you all, every bit I can send,

Your young old soldier Tommy.

16 June. . . . I wish you would send me some safety pins to hold up my kilt. I wear nothing under my kilt but I pin my shirt between my legs. Don't send the pins too large, yes large and small mixed. . . .

I am doing my best to live the life of the men around me – I am no longer the Peter of yesterday or a week ago. I can swear and laugh at the most awful coarse jokes. I am a Tommy by jove. You won't know me when I come on leave. . . .

22 June. . . . I love these marches in the semi-twilight, through narrow lanes and dusty highways – a soldier's life suits me immensely. I am as brown and weather-beaten as ever I have been and feel very fit. . . . I can imagine you and my darling wee family sitting in the garden having tea. . . .

In July McGregor made a surprise visit to his family after he had been picked, together with a sergeant and two corporals, for a week's recruiting in Edinburgh ('marching up and down the streets trying to pick up men'). He wrote to his sister Nell, in Chelsea:

There is quite a recruiting drive going on in this town just now – everybody is cracking up their respective regiments as hard as they can. . . . Folks take a new fancy to you when you wear the King's uniform. I have met people who would only stiffly nod, now they wave their hands to you – and want to do Princes Street in your company. Such is life!

27 August. . . . We had a ripping march last night – 12 miles in full marching kit. Before we started the Major said – Any man who does not feel able for the march take one step forward – not one fell out. Away we went – grand – braw Scots lads with the kilts flying and the band playing. We started at 7 o'clock and arrived home at 11.

It was great marching along the roads, passing through villages with staring crowds of folk watching us – the boys sang and called to the girls – and the folks laughed and shouted to us. The moon was full and shone on us with its steady stare and we tramped on and on – the roads were feet thick in dust – we went up and down hill, over all kinds of roads, through dells so dark that we couldn't see the man in front. I thought of you, and wondered if you would be looking at the moon. . . .

You should hear how the chaps talk about the girls here, and what they do to them. One told me two of them had tea in a house near here kept by two widows – after tea they turned out to be – guess what! Another chap told me they had a girl in a field. Two of them – think of it! I am going out tomorrow afternoon, I am going for a walk, and will think of you all the time. You are the only person I care about, and love you always.

I was so glad to get your letter. You are a stupid darling to be so run down and not able to sleep – I could shake you – what's the use of worrying – things will come all right never fear. . . . Love to my dear family, kiss them over and over again – and also your dear self and try to go to sleep. Think I am bothering you like I used to do – and you will soon go to sleep – you dear old thing. . . .

5 September. . . . It makes my heart turn round when you say you love me. I don't think it matters how old one is – you can always love – at least I can – and it's always you. I haven't spoken to a woman since I left you – apart from Nell in London – that's not bad for me is it? . . .

8 September. [After a mass parade inspected by King George V] . . . I couldn't see much of the King – the sun was shining in my eyes all the time. It was a great sight to see thousands of troops massed together. We were the only kilted Battalion on parade and we did look well. One or 2 fell out – it's queer but the men are very young, I am sure I am the oldest man in the Battalion. . . .

10 September. [After visiting his brother-in-law Charlie, who was in the same battalion, in hospital, suffering from piles] . . . One soldier was surrounded by girls – when I came past his bed he said 'Here, Jock, we're discussing whether you wear anything under your kilt?' I whispered to him will I lift it up, and he turned to the girls and said 'He'll lift it up if you like' – but I escaped out of the doors. These Tommies don't stand upon ceremony, everything is above board, they have no modesty at all. We all swear at each other – call each other awful names – but we are good chaps nevertheless. I send you all my love, you dear old thing – I would love to kiss you.

24 October. Aldershot, Surrey. . . . We are going to be worked to the last ounce of endurance, out all day and night. We are preparing for war and no mistake – up at 5.20, lights out at 10.15. And the grub scanty. Think of us tramping over hills in all kinds of weather. . . .

When we left camp at 9.00 yesterday the mist was so thick that we couldn't see the man in front of us. When we got into the road I thought every moment we would be run

8

down by some huge army transport waggon drawn by those huge steam road engines. We stood on the left side of the road for more than 20 minutes before we moved on – and to see rows and rows of soldiers and ASC waggons and artillery passing us was weird in the extreme – they loomed out of the mist with men swearing and tugging at mules' heads – engines drawing huge waggons laden with food for the army – looming out of the mist and disappearing into it.

Some of our Platoon behind us began to sing 'Annie Laurie' and 'Maxwelton Braes are Bonny' and I was never so near to tears – and homesick and Jensick and familysick and had the most horrible feelings. I stood there in the mist and wanted to be home. At last we moved on and the day cheered up, the sun came out and I stuck it. . . .

21 November. Whitley Camp, Milford, Surrey. . . . We had tea in a swell tea room in Guildford – officers galore with their women folk – it seems to me soldiers wherever they go manage to pick up women – our men are no sooner in a place than you see them with girls.

Your dear sweet letter was perfect. I love you to tell me your feelings towards me. I love you exactly the same way – at night I lie in the dark and see you quite distinctly. Oh! I do love you then: but in such a nice way. My poor old heart feels very sore, and terribly anxious about you. Well, cheer up – what's the use of going sad? I love you now – and think of you sweetly, and just the way you want me to – Dear old thing. I want all your love, and my wee family's too. . . .

25 November. . . . We were having a shot at manning trenches and jumping out of them – charging others, sticking our bayonets into sacks – and rushing on and sticking them into bags hanging between posts. You

9

remember Bob laughing at soldiers doing the same at a cinema we went to.

I was running at these trenches, not very hard I must say – I was last, as one of the chaps gave me a kick in the stomach when jumping out which knocked me back in the trench. I came on last when (I was told this afterwards) Mr McDonald, one of our officers, said 'Hurry up McGregor, don't run like a broken-hearted jockey' – this went round all the company and they were just laughing like anything – in fact I was doing a bayonet charge all by myself and the chaps were standing roaring and laughing at my fierce charge which I was doing alone.

One time I got stuck in a trench. I tripped over a sack and my pack got stuck and I had an awful job getting free but when I did – by Jove – it was quite fun and I enjoyed it immensely. We are a lot of babies and enjoy life in full measure – war never enters our minds. . . .

26 November. . . . I was so pleased with Bob's letter and sketches. Dear wee man, I am quite sure he will be your prop – will look after you – he is lucky to have such a fine mother. I do think he will be a credit to you – of course so will my sweet wee daughter – she is perfect, the dear little woman. . . .

5 December. This will be a short note just to say I am wild with joy at coming home at the end of this week. I was never so happy in my life – I can hardly do anything but think and dream day-dreams of what we will do on my furlough. How short the time will be – but never mind – we will make every moment a year and never – never – will I leave you all the time – I will just hug and kiss you and my sweet dear wee family. . . .

18 December. Here I am back in camp, safe and sound –

it's a wonder though, the train was packed with soldiers going to camp and to the front – they were in every condition – sober, half-drunk and full drunk. The drink that was consumed on the train must have been that of a good-sized public house. I never saw the like of it. I had about three inches of a seat – chaps were sitting all over me. I don't think I slept one wink – chaps were sick all round – still with all they were a cheery crowd – and just what you would expect at this time.

I was glad when we got to King's Cross. We got down to the Tube to Waterloo. These Tubes were crowded – we could hardly get in – we seemed to cause great interest – wild, half-asleep or half-drunk Highlanders bursting into tube carriages. . . .

It's an awful job leaving your family – I felt it worse this time – everything is so uncertain. However here I am once more and will soon shake down to the routine of camp life. I have lit my pipe – well I wish I had been lighting it at the fire in the children's room with you sitting on the other side and my wee family near at hand to come and give me a few kisses – not to say my dear wife. . . .

26 December. . . . I so loved your dear letter this morning – you dear old thing to be so much in love – I wonder why – and so it is for ever and ever – and so it is for me – I couldn't be more in love than I am, you dear old sweetheart. I do hope the family had a jolly time and that Santa Claus filled their stockings to their liking. I think it is the first Xmas I have spent away from home. Never mind I was with you all the time – cheer up – things will come all right and we will have a rare time. . . .

1 January 1916. [After the Company's Hogmanay dinner.] . . . The Colonel came at 11.20, then I was called upon by the chairman to propose the Colonel's toast. I got up feeling

fine and delivered my speech. I enclose it.

'Major Petter, officers, NCO's and comrades. I have been asked to propose the health of our Colonel, Colonel Macdonald. We all know him – his stately presence – his soldierly bearing on parade and in the field. Under all circumstances we have his calm serene quietly moving figure – that marks him as a man we are proud to be led by. He has our welfare at heart and I can truly say – what would the 14th A and S H be without its Colonel, and what would our Colonel be without his A and S H. To my mind, and I am sure to us all, they are inseparable.

'Sir, in calling upon my comrades to drink your very good health I shall say – may you long have strength to blow your whistle – and – I can assure you – at these sounds and signs every man will follow you – to the end if need be. Comrades, the Colonel.'

The chaps said it was fine – they all congratulated me – I got tremendous shouts at various points as the speech went on – and at the end they yelled themselves hoarse. They all said it was the best speech of the evening. I felt pleased with myself – for once. I was very much surprised at even being asked to do it – I wonder how it came about – I should like to know.

We came back to our huts – the place was simply pandemonium – chaps came in from other huts with bottles – whisky, burgundy, sherry – I took a mouthful of burgundy out of a bottle when the New Year came in. What a noise we made then – a great many were drunk. We shook hands – we wished a good New Year to everybody.

I thought of you when I was giving my speech – I am sure you were round somewhere. I know you are looking after me all the time – you dear old thing. . . .

20 January. . . . I got your dear letter and loved it and read it over and over. . . . I was thinking if I get leave again,

that is before I go to the front, I will worry you all over again – I will have my honeymoon, a new honeymoon, I will love you – love you – I will never let you out of my sight one instant. . . .

23 January. . . . I had such a lovely dream about you last night. I awoke still holding you tightly in my arms. Oh how I loved you – just everything happened – as if you had really been there – you were my own darling wife – I was having my own darling wife – it was sweet. I read your last letter in bed last night before lights out – perhaps that's why – it's the first love I have had since I left you – you dear old darling sweetheart wife – of course I love to hear you say loving things to me. Do you ever dream of me loving you – every bit of you being loved by me? I loved my dream last night. . . .

1 February. I think this has been the saddest day of my soldiering. Our dear old Colonel has bid us farewell – he leaves on account of his age – the War Office won't let him have command of his beloved Battalion.

It was a most affecting scene. The whole Battalion was paraded in full dress – dressed up on 3 sides of a square – and he (the Colonel) made his farewell speech – then we gave three cheers and were dismissed. The proceedings didn't last longer than ten minutes, yet in those minutes the poor old fellow lived a lifetime – he could hardly speak – and the men were very much affected too – some had tears in their eyes. It is surprising how attached you get to a man – and we all adore the Colonel. The name of our new one is Colonel Gunn. . . .

7 March. The worst shock since I joined the army, to think of my dear old ancient darling being in bed ill. I am just one large mass of concern, can't do anything sort of feeling,

when I think of my dear old darling being upset – in fact I was so down in the mouth that I dropped my watch and have injured it internally – it won't go. . . .

23 April. Blackdown Camp, Farnborough, Hants. . . . I was standing in the High Street, Camberley, last night talking to some chaps, when a bunch of girls closed round us, and one put her arm round my waist. I was so angry. I talked to her sharply – called her impertinent – the chaps simply roared with laughter, and of course when I came back to the hut Anderson told the story with variations. I was very much ragged by the chaps – they thought it a huge joke. . . .

27 April. . . . Our attack was from one trench to another, we had to rush across – about 80 yards – and cut down a barbed wire entanglement. I was a bomber, I carried a sack of sand bombs. When I got to the barbed wire I was told I was a casualty, so I lay down in the sun and dozed. I was quite glad to be a casualty. It was glorious lying in the sun – the sky was hazy with heat – there was I basking in the sun while the fighting passed over me. . . .

6 May. . . . How I love and long for you – it's almost five months since I was here – a mighty long time to be without your wife – especially if you love her – and I do, darling – I just adore you, I think you are the best, dearest living soul in the world, and such a brave woman. What will you do without me – if I am knocked out? Marry again? Oh my darling – never mind, I have had much of your sweetness – and I want more – heaps more – I want a new honeymoon, I want to kiss you all – just like when we were first married – I would love to hold you in my arms – just Jen, my darling wife. You mustn't say anything, I will kiss you all the time – so there! – dearest. . . .

8 May. . . . I wrote such a loving letter to you yesterday – for your own dear self. I had to write it darling so please don't be angry with me. I longed for you so much. It was the only way I could cure myself. . . .

9 May. . . . I remember a nice little story about you, it is this: when I was at Whitley Camp we used to have attacks on a little house – empty it was and the garden was all overgrown. In a corner grew a rose tree, the roses were just on the turn – their colour was heliotrope turning to dark brown purple – one of them hanging with a sweet drooping head – very much alone – the petals were just turning in. I said – 'That's my Jen' it was so like you – I wanted to take it in my arms (hands) but I couldn't get near for a barbed wire fence. I am sure I would have found two buds – that I am sure of – your darling children. How I longed to kiss that rose – to touch it. I dreamed of it. . . .

There is a chance of my being home on Saturday or Sunday – it depends when we finish our shooting. . . .

21 May. Here I am back in camp. You are never out of my thoughts all the time. I was so sad to leave you and my darling wee children. I was quite struck down with their grown-upness. The way they went about things – just as grown up as we are. . . .

31 May. I think we leave on Saturday or Sunday morning. It's come at last, my own darling sweet wife. This will be the worst time for you – but cheer up. Don't be down – things will come all right – fate has been working hard with me. There is one thing, I seem to love you deeper and better than I have ever done. . . .

4 June. I am away at last. . . . I love you all with a devour-

15

ing love. I think of you all the time and can only hope that things will turn out for the best. Fate is a queer thing – here I am – and so must go.

Farewell my dear darling sweet wife.

Pete.

McGregor wrote forty-two letters to his wife during his thirteen weeks at the front up to the day he was killed. Under the shadow of the censor, they are discreetly addressed to 'My dear Jen' or 'My dear wife', and his 'devouring love' finds little expression. But that this reticence would have come as no surprise to his wife seems evident from an allusion in his first letter: 'The strain of this note has to be very circumspect – as you know – but it's all there, more than ever before.'

There were lengthy spells away from the firing line when McGregor had leisure enough to indulge his day-dreams of home and to wish that Jen could have been with him to enjoy the 'very paintable' French countryside. The tiny sketchbook he asked for in his first letter from Plymouth has, indeed, survived with the letters, a few of its pages adorned with his neat pencil sketches of corners of a farmyard, a church spire in trees.

The trenches under shellfire were a nightmare he was quite unprepared for. 'Rats in a hole hounded out with shot and shell' was scarcely what he had envisaged when he had seen himself, before enlistment, 'giving a good account of myself in the field of battle'. These letters give a chilling impression of the dehumanised carnage that much of the war had become. Not once in his letters does McGregor mention having sighted one of the enemy or even of firing a shot from his rifle.

McGregor uses vague 'Somewhere in France' headings to his letters – 'A cowshed', 'A ruined cottage', 'The big house', 'The tent', 'Reserve trenches', 'Firing line' – and his exact whereabouts on the Western Front is likely to have remained a mystery to his wife. From 1 July she would have read in the

16

*papers of the great Allied offensive on the Somme and may have
been unaware that all the time her husband's battalion was
engaged in static sectors of the front some distance to the north.
Only his last letter – referring to slag heaps and the ruins of a
town where 'a furious battle was fought last September' –
clearly identifies the coal-mining area around Loos.*

*Apart from an allusion to 'the distant rumble of big guns that
for nights have been making the earth tremble in my tent',
McGregor shows no awareness of the bloody fighting in progress
on the Somme. His fate was to be a passive victim of that dev-
astating war of attrition in which routine and indiscriminate
artillery barrages claimed far more lives than all the 'death or
glory' assaults over no-man's-land, and which added a new
word to the military vocabulary: shellshock. Only once did
McGregor apparently lose his nerve. What he barely gives a
hint of is the impression he made on his comrades – 'a centre of
cheerfulness and good humour'.*

*From his arrival in France on 6 June 1916 it took only nine
days for McGregor to experience his 'baptism of shrapnel'.
Extracts from early letters indicate his buoyant progress to the
front:*

I am sitting in a farmyard somewhere in France. How
peaceful it is, men writing, hens with large families of little
chickens, a grand looking cock strutting about, one chap
washing his shirt at the pump. The folk were coming out of
the kirk just like in Scotland rigged up in their best
clothes. . . . I haven't had my clothes off since I left Blackdown. I have to sleep in them – funny me an old soldier. I
laugh at myself often – the quiet wee man living the warlike
life. . . .

I am keeping up the tradition of the family – nothing
seems to knock me over. I may be sort of a slow soldier, but
what can you expect at my age. I am cheerful and hope to

be cheerful when the time comes for the great thing. . . .

Last night I went down to the town and had a lovely dinner. The French seem to know how to cook. There were six of us, and we had two bottles of wine – think of me drinking wine. . . .

The ancient Angelus is everywhere. I saw the picture in a field yesterday – an old woman and a man – she stood hands folded in front, head bowed, her man standing working a longhandled fork and the rain pouring down on them as it was on us. Was she praying for us as 'the Deliverer' or the good God for sending the rain. . .

. . . You should have seen us in the cattle trucks, we were just lying all over the place – so mixed up that I am sure no one could separate us one from the other. We passed through some beautiful scenery, no one would think there was such a thing as war – folks went about their work sedately, didn't even make a wave as we passed. British troops passing somewhere in France don't excite as they used to do. . . .

15 June. Under Shell Fire. We came up today, marching quite 13 miles over the most awful roads – my heels are tired with the constant tramp on the cobbles. When we came near the Germans opened fire on us and gave us our baptism of shrapnel. By Jove, to say I had no fear would be a lie. I was full of fear. We heard the whistle of the shells as they came towards us and then the sharp nasty crack as they exploded. The order was given to down, which we did in double quick time. I am glad to say no one was hurt.

This village is simply knocked to pieces by the shell-fire – it's awful to look at. But there are many of the folks still in their houses. . . . I am sitting in the room of a deserted house – we are to lie on a stone floor – it is very cold. I am quite well – my fear has all gone. The chaps walk about laughing and talking as if nothing is going on. I will soon

18

get the same spirit I hope. . . .

17 June. Firing Line. I am sitting on the fire step, with shells flying overhead, at the real front at last. Thinking is a difficult matter here, everything gets knocked out of your head by the infernal noise. I have been looking at the white blank page of this letter for a long time. . . .

We travelled miles of trenches to reach the point we occupy. Some of the places we passed were liquid mud up to our knees. The town we passed through was an absolute ruin, not a house that is not blown to bits [Ypres?]. I never saw the like of it, not a soul anywhere. I can't describe the look it has. It made me shiver – wooden crosses on the roadside and in places in the town marking the heroes' death – what devastation – a day of judgement more like. Man builds and then builds machines to destroy, well he seems to have made a better job of destroying this town. I'll never forget it. . . .

21 June. I am all right – just the same as ever – but no – that can never be. The four days we were in the trenches has turned me upside down. No man can experience such things and come out the same.

We were in the front line of the trenches. Places that are bashed down and built up at the same time, sleeping on a fire platform step, if that is possible, hard at work all the time – stand-to – fatigue parties going out at all times – dodging all kinds of infernal machines – things that can swallow you up – and now here I am sitting smoking the pipe of peace in front of 'the Ruin'. . . .

This morning I was awoken by a most terrible roar – one of our guns or a Hun shell perhaps – I thought I was in the trenches – it was only a chap banging on a tin tray to waken us for breakfast. . . .

25 June. Front Line Trenches. . . . We took our positions in the firing line trenches. I was one of a guard – I was in a narrow hole – so narrow that I had to squeeze myself very thin to move at all. The sky looked very angry, black as ink. The Hun as usual was straffing like anything – flinging all kinds of horrible things that made awful noises when they burst, it's a wonder I am here to tell the tale – however nature thought she would have a go.

Lightning and thunder and torrents of rain came on – I have never seen such lightning, zig-zag flashes that looked as if they would blow up the whole world, then the rain. Our narrow hole became somewhat uncomfortable, the rain poured in mixed with the earth. I was soon covered with a wet sticky covering – the water in the trench came up over my boots – and there I stayed with six of my fellow soldiers keeping guard – what a night that was, rain and mud above – and mud and water below. In the morning I did not feel at all happy and told our sergeant, the officer of the watch sent me off. I went down to the cooks' place and spent the rest of the day there, a most miserable one indeed. . . .

Our first experience of war hasn't been happy – our company has by far the worst end of the stick – we must be thought a hardy crew. I can't say why we were taken at first into one of the most dangerous, hottest, places on our front – perhaps it was to try us. 'The Trenches' – who will ever write about them – tell the truth. . . . The air is full of dreadful noises. The night is like a night at the 'marine gardens' – all kinds of flash lights are put up at intervals so that no one can travel over without being seen – there is a feeling of nerves all over – a restless agitated spirit is over all. . . .

29 June. . . . Our spell in the trenches was rather strenuous – the weather was awful – rain turned the trenches into mud baths. German shot and shell – you don't look out for

a dry place to flop down in – down you go in the first seemingly safe spot, deep in mud and water you may be sure.
When you rise up you are soaking wet, however you have
for the moment saved your life. . . .

A 'Rum Jar', the largest Hun shell known on our front,
can knock in yards of trenches, so you can see if you are not
sort of smart you have a chance of being buried. I have
never heard anything like my experiences, words will never
give it, it is terrible. We are rats in a hole hounded out with
shot and shell. You can't go to sleep, you are on the move
all the time. . . .

Last Sunday was a day I will never forget – much of our
trenches were blown in – I had taken up my place on a fire
step and was taking off my boots to wipe my feet with a
groundsheet bag. I was sitting there writing to you – bare
feet and all – when I heard a peculiar noise behind me.
When I looked round I saw a 'Rum Jar' – it looked like the
side of a house, falling out of the sky. I made a wild dash
away from it, knocked my boots into the water and mud,
fell down in the bottom of the trench – then hell was let
loose. The shock was awful – the sky was darkened by the
shower of earth and stone – it fell all round me. I was an
awful sight after – well – I was all right – I put on my boots
and socks as they were.

I found that the trench had been blown in and that I
couldn't get along to my section – however I climbed over
the top. My rifle was gone – buried with a few other things
– I got them later when the trench was dug out. To look
back on it is amusing, but for the time you are scared to
death. . . .

*A letter dated 4 July, three days after the launching of the
Somme offensive, brought good news for Jen:*
Today the Battalion was under orders to proceed to some-

where. At the last moment our company was kept behind to act as guards etc. to the Corps that is coming in. We will be in this job for a month, so you needn't worry about me for a month. I will not be near the firing line or the trenches.

Apart from guard duties, McGregor's company was occupied with general fatigues – sweeping the streets, shifting coal, carting dung from farmyards to fields. He called the village where they were billeted in tents 'our haven of refuge'.

. . . We seem to be out of the way of everything, life is very quiet. The painter would flourish here – some of the best farmyards are extremely paintable. The landscape around is very fine, flat with rows of trees. Red-roofed farms are built in the form of a square, the dwelling-house is at one corner, then come out-houses, and in the middle of the square – a dirty filthy midden. When some of this has to be shifted – well, I suggest they might heave it at the Hun, they might retreat a little faster. . . .

I wish you could see me in the evening going into the town having a feast with a large bottle of red wine to wash it down. I am becoming a bad old toper. . . .

If it wasn't for being dressed in a uniform I would say I was on holiday – all I want is you and the family. . . .

I went to the Parish Church on Sunday. The place was crowded with villagers in their Sunday best. The singing was very loud and the organ most untuneful, however the eye was charmed. The Curé's sermon I have no doubt was good, his French was so nice to listen to – I didn't understand very much all the same. . . .

Tell Bob to write one of his stories for me. Tell him that I don't forget him – and that he is looking after you and Margaret. I asked him to do all this – poor wee chap. I have a

22

Hun bullet for him. . . .

It was after three weeks, rather than a month, that McGregor was back among the ruins and the shellfire. His last eighteen letters find him in and out of the front line, increasingly wishing the war was ending ('it's horrible – there is something wrong somewhere').

24 July. Ruined Village. . . . There is nobody in the village – most of the houses are smashed – gardens all overgrown. I believe near here is a huge cherry tree with lovely cherries – but none of us dare go near to get them as it is marked by the Hun snipers. The Hun bullets whizz all over the place.

I wish you could see this house – everything broken – no windows – no doors. I went through the garden – weeds everywhere. I cut a rose – the most beautiful deep crimson, what a Beauty it is – I wish I could send it to you. What a shame to see things like they are. . . .

26 July. [After accompanying a night wiring party into No Man's Land.] . . . The ground between the lines was covered with large shell holes. I was always falling into them – the other chaps knew the job and didn't seem to care – they went on with the work standing. The Hun star shells are very bright, they light up the place like a strong electric lamp – that's the time you have to stand quite still. . . .

1 August. In the Firing Line. . . . The wild flowers grow all over the place – I enclose a scarlet pimpernel, I plucked it from one of the sandbags on the parapet. I will send it to you right from in front of the Huns. . . . I am melting with the heat. Thank Grannie for the oatcakes. . . .

6 August. . . . The whole front line was awake throughout the night. We never know when the Hun might take it into his head to visit us so we wait and watch. The night was very bright, cold and clear – the stars shone – I watched them change their position – it's queer to think that [illegible] thousands and thousands [illegible] and yet this drop in the universe can't live in peace with itself. All night the sound of rifles, the rattle of machine guns and the constant sending up of star shells, which made everything like day for a short time – went out and left things darker than before.

The country here is very flat, when I stand on the firestep I can see miles and miles of open flat country – green fields – the mark of our trenches seems to run every-where. . . .

I often wish I was brave but when the Hun begins straff-ing my nerves get worked up – it's a nervous job dodging things in a hole in the ground. The rats and mice run all over the place. One little mouse this morning made friends with me – it was such a nice little chap – he ran in and out of the holes along the sandbags in front of me – it was stand-to, half an hour before dawn. I was quite glad to see him. . . .

13 August. We came down to this comparatively quiet place last night. Last weekend we had a terrible time in the firing line. So bad that we only spent three nights and days instead of the four we should have done. Last Sunday the Hun kept us lively most of the day – the Devil seemed to know that the 'Jocks' were in. I almost melted in the heat rushing along the trench. You could hear the call from one of us 'Rum Jar on the left' and the men rush to the right – wobble-wobble-wobble – Thump – and then the explosion – with dense volumes of smoke, you could see nothing for

some minutes.

We had two periscopes shot to bits by snipers – out of the wreck of the two I made a periscope which turned out excellent. I don't know what we should have done without it – you daren't show your head above the parapet – the snipers at the spot are dashed good shots.

We got dozens of sandbags and put them on during the night. In the morning the Hun thought something was on – at about 6 a.m. they began to sling the D–able Jars of high explosives – before breakfast they slung over no less than 52 – we had about 100 yards of trench and these Jars fell here, there and everywhere – how we weren't laid out is a mystery to me – providence was on our side, sure.

We had another spell before dinner – and then our most melancholy time was at tea-time. Tea was almost over when 'Jars' came over again – one very close – I was on guard – one of our chaps came rushing out of the next bay – 'Stretchers quick' – 'Who is it?' I called – 'Jock Burns' – 'Badly?' – 'Yes! – out!' I could say nothing but 'O Christ' – I never felt so miserable in my life – Jock Burns, such a nice young boy.

When the stretcher came round with its burden, there lay poor Jock – I could say nothing – I had two drops of his blood on my hand for two days. Nobody can say how he got knocked out – a small piece of shrapnel must have hit him – gone right through him – it was a merciful, instantaneous death. I saw him three minutes before and was telling him to cheer up – 'It's all right, Jock, it's war you know' – then the call for the stretcher. . . .

24 August. . . . I was glad you wrote to the boy's mother – it is rotten for her. I think the saddest part of all was on the dump that same evening. There he was laying on the stretcher made ready to be taken away to his last resting place – they wrap you up in your waterproof sheet – keep on, as far

25

as I could see, all your clothes – like the brave of old – ready to take his place at the sound of the bugle – it's a soldier's way of doing things. There were many more going down to the same place – that never to be forgotten night – it was a queer scene altogether. . . .

I am sure you will be having a good time at Burntisland – how the kiddies will enjoy the sea and the shore – how I long to be with you. I remember the long stretches of sand – how lovely it was. We see sometimes the *Sketch* and the *Mirror* – but I laugh at the fake photographs of the boys at the front – perhaps the folk at home would rather have the laughing Tommy, doing his duty, always smiling. . . .

31 August. I haven't had a bath for ages. I am getting used to it – my knees are a dirty brown – my neck must be black as a schoolboy's, a beautiful ring round it – I even got the order to get my hair cut – I must be an awful looking sight. I had a lice hunt this forenoon and oh my I caught thousands – quite big fat ones and wee fellows – they get into the folds of your kilt and down the seams of your shirt – the devils. Nothing kills them – powdering has no effect – the only way is to heave a few Rum Jars at them. The best joke is I have been wearing the little bags you sent to me ages ago – today I looked into the folds and found whole families dwelling there. The only way to keep them down is to hunt them every day. . . .

P.S. I wonder if it would hurt Grannie's feelings if you told her not to send so many oatcakes. I am in one place for so short a time and to carry extra weight is just a bit too much for me. . . .

McGregor's last letter, concluded on 12 September, the day before he was killed, was the longest for some time (over 1200 words). It was written in the reserve trenches after a quiet spell in the firing line that he seems actually to have enjoyed:

. . . We made our dugout for two a nice little house – I pinched some planks from around about our door and floored the place, this made it warm for our beds at night. We slept like tops – it was a pain to have to waken when called for our time on guard. Time didn't hang on your hands – the weather was ideal – the nights so clear – it was a pleasure to look over the top – to look at no man's land in the moonlight – to watch the effects of star shells on the landscape. Occasionally some fireworks came over – scattering bits of shrapnel – but luckily did no harm.

I was sad to leave our happy dugout – what a place we are in now – deep dugouts that hold many men – have more than one entrance. I am sure that we are more than twelve feet underground – the place is dark, dirty, the supports of the roof are black with the smoke of ages, the floors filthy, large stones all over the place, you have to scrape a place to lay your body. A candle burns all night to keep away the rats – rats as big as cats wander up and down – eat your grub – worry everything you leave. The 'Hamelin' chap would have plenty to do here. . . .

The final passage of the letter, with its prophetic reflection on the casualness of death on the Western Front, must have had an unbearable poignancy for his darling Jen:

. . . I got your letter and the poems, very nice indeed. How I long for Scotland and the 'Green Fields of England' – oh to be in dear old Edinburgh – it's the loveliest place on this earth.

I am well, and am looking forward to the end of the war. I wish it would hurry up. I don't know!! It's a queer state of affairs altogether – one of our men was caught by a sniper – he was standing at the entrance of his dugout – the bullet went in under his shoulder – alas! alas! . . .

I am now sitting in my dingy dirty dugout. I have been down to our stores in the village behind our reserve trenches, on a 'ration fatigue'. When I was standing at the cook-house door – the cook-house is a ruined house in the High Street – I saw the stretcher coming to take away the poor fellow who was 'sniped'. How sad that was – it was melancholy – he was carried out, wrapped up in his water-proof sheet, placed on the thing and whisked away.

His passing didn't seem to cause much stir – crowds of chaps were standing about – of course we all came to attention as it passed – that was all. The business of the hour had to go on. A dead man is no use to the army, get him out of the way as quickly as possible.

War is a terrible thing and so few realise it.

I helped to carry the grub up, and I am now going to settle down for the night. I am the only one in the dug-out – the rest are out on fatigue.

Good night.

From Captain A.H.Miller, 'B' Company.

On the afternoon of the 13th your husband was working with several others in a reserve trench. Suddenly the Germans began to shell the trench and I very much regret to say that your husband was struck down. He died almost at once and suffered no pain. All that it was possible to do was done and he was taken to the dressing station within a very few minutes of his being struck. He died a soldier's death doing his duty for King and Country.

We buried him last night in the British Soldiers' Cemetery. It was a beautiful evening and the simple service was held while the guns were booming round us. The cemetery is a pretty spot, but I'm sorry I cannot tell you the name of the place at present. . . .

Your husband was the life of the whole Company, he was always so cheerful, however hard the work, and he always got a laugh from the men with his jokes and sayings. He was a most invaluable man to have out here. His loss will be felt not only by this Company but the whole Battalion, in which he was very well known.

From Lt Col G. Gunn, C O of the Battalion:
. . . Your husband was a credit to his Regiment and his Country. . . .

From Major H.B. Murdoch, C O of 'B' Company:
. . . He was universally beloved in the Battalion and a very wide circle of officers and men are mourning his loss, one which is personal to themselves. He was a willing and trust-worthy soldier and was always cheerful, indeed he was as it were a centre of cheerfulness and good humour in the Company. . . .

From the Revd B.D.Anderson, Battalion Chaplain:
. . . Your husband was a great favourite, one of the best known men in his Company. After many a weary day he cheered his comrades and he had always a pleasant smile for the Padre. Even in death his smile was pleasant to see. . . .

From Private C. Holroyd (McGregor's brother-in-law):
. . . I never had a brother and, especially since being out here, Pete was that and more to me. His good humour, cheery word and ready joke never failed us and often when we have been 'dead to the world' a word from him would buck us up and we would carry on. But you who know him better than anyone will know all this. . . .

29

He was laid to rest yesterday evening at 6.30. It was a lovely evening and just at the time there was a beautiful rainbow in the sky. I had a wee sprig of Scotch heather in my pocket book and this I placed on the grave. It was all I had or could get.

The last words I heard Pete say as we were leaving our dugout to commence work were 'Hurry up, boys, or we shall get something else to carry.' Dear Jen, I feel as though I had not taken proper care of Pete, and yet what could I do? Give my love to Margaret and Bobby, to you my whole heart goes out in sympathy. Would that I could do more.

Robert McGregor, who was nine at the time, can remember the day the news of his father's death was broken to his mother. 'We were staying at the home of an old aunt and my mother was in an upstairs room cleaning out the canary cage. I was surprised to see Aunt Helen and Aunt Kitty walking up the terrace. Somehow the news had reached my grandfather before my mother and they had come to break it to her. I followed them upstairs and through the closed door heard them crying. It was a shattering blow to mother. She had a breakdown and went to stay with a sister in London.'

As he had promised his father as a small boy, Bob McGregor looked after his mother all her life. She lived with him, for much of the time in Essex, until her death in 1946. And it is thanks to him that the letters are now preserved in the archives of the Imperial War Museum. He had known that they were hidden away in a large suitcase, but it was not until 1968 that he started reading them. He then spent many weeks copying them out, word for word, into sixteen exercise books (pasting on one page the scarlet pimpernel his father had picked in that front-line trench).

'My mother used to read extracts from the letters to Margaret

and me,' he recalls. 'But reading them all through was a revelation. I was deeply moved. It was like a voice coming to me. I could understand his feelings, his enthusiasms. I think we are quite alike. I was even told once by an aunt that my voice was very like his.

'My memories of my father are faint. We lived in a large 1826 terrace house in Great Stuart Street in the west end of Edinburgh. I remember that he could be quite strict and stern while teaching my sister and me the three R's (presumably to save school fees). But we were a very close affectionate family. My last memory is of the day he left us after his final leave. Margaret and I came to the tram stop and he waved back to us from the open top of the tram-car. Mother was too upset to come with us – she had said her goodbyes indoors.'

McGregor finds nothing strange in his father's transformation from organist and choirmaster into Tommy. 'Inbred in most Scotsmen is a love of roughing it, of living out. I suppose it's a kind of folk memory going back to the clan days. My father's great concern about me was that I should 'be a man'. My mother told me he used to say 'Playing the piano is not a man's job.' The last thing he wanted me to become was a musician. And I have no doubt he would have been disappointed that I did become a professional artist – an illustrator.'

Of the father he only dimly remembers and the mother he remained close to throughout her life he says: 'They were extremely attached to each other. I don't remember that my mother read over the letters again, it would have been too painful, but she was constantly talking about him. Marrying again never entered her head.'

Jen McGregor's voice can be heard again in the seven last letters she wrote to her 'darling husband', or 'darling boy', four of them after he had been killed, which were returned to her with his other effects.

They are lively with the trivia of her daily doings and warm with loving concern. But the images they leave are of a tragic

31

*sitting by her fireside, the children in bed, opposite
chair; preening herself, in a fetching new outfit, in
he mirror, imagining Pete's admiring gaze, not
knowing that he was dead.*

. . . I always mean to say about not saying loving things in
your letters – I know they are there and that you are loving
us more than ever. I could say more than I do, but I am
afraid lest I make you more homesick than ever if I pour
out too much of my loving feelings – so I try and tell you all
the everyday things I know will interest you. . . .

I am longing for you to come and give me a hug. . .

You seem to be getting used to things now. You are a
marvellous person. I can't think how you've stood it all so
well. I suppose you would shut that mouth and stick out
that stubborn chin and just 'stick it'. . . .

Last night when I was kissing Bob goodnight he said
'Goodnight darling, you really are an *excellent* mother, just
like a turkey'! When we were at Burntisland a brood of
ducklings was being mothered by a turkey because they
make the best mothers. Margaret said tonight she adored
me and no matter how much I scolded her it made no difference in her love. They always put up a little prayer for
Daddy to be kept safe and come home to them all
right. . . .

My brains are dull and stupid and refuse to work tonight
– if I only had you sitting beside me on the sofa what a lot I
should have to say to you. How I long for that time. . . .

Poor old darling. How I do love you and long to see you.
I am such a swell when I get on my 'glad rags' – my brown
coat and skirt, brown shoes and striking blue hat with
brown feathers. I really am quite smart and up to date. My
dress is a little short and my shoes are very smart. I hope
you will come home while they are still looking nice. . . .

*Tragically it is the letter she began writing on the day he w\
killed, 13 September, that expresses the deepest concern,\
coupled with a guilty feeling that she herself was not 'suffering\
enough':*

My darling Husband,

Your letter dated 8th came this morning. I was very glad to
get it but sorry to hear you were back in the beastly
trenches again. You don't acknowledge the parcel I posted
on the 4th, I wonder if you got it all right. Perhaps you
would get it in the trenches – that would be all right, you
would be glad of the things. It is beginning to be cold here
now. I wonder if you are feeling it too. It will be pretty bad
for you when it gets really cold, you will have to let me
know when you want things sent.

Bob is getting very keen on his stamps, he works at them
for a long time now, it is very good for him. He is good as
gold when he is busy. He is getting to be a fine bold laddie
– so clean and nice in spite of small sins – I adore him sometimes. . . .

It's ten o'clock now so I must be stopping. Good night
my dear old man I wonder when you and I will sit one on
each side of the fire like Darby and Joan again!

Thursday. It is so cold we have spent all the forenoon
sitting over the fire. I hope you will let me know when you
want anything sent – gloves or anything – but perhaps you
are not having it quite so cold as we are.

I wonder what you are doing poor old darling – I am
always thinking about you. It seems terrible that you
should be there in the middle of all that while I sit in peace
and quiet comfort at home. I suppose it's just to let your
wives and bairns do that that you are all suffering like that.
I don't feel as if I suffered enough – except for the continual

33

anxiety about you. I don't have to suffer at all, one would never know that a war was going on at all.

You seem to be getting my letters all right anyway and you have never missed a parcel. Sall was very sorry you'd had Charlie's parcel to carry and said you should just have opened it and eaten the contents!

We have had dinner and everyone feels sleepy so I am going to sit before the drawing room fire and read.

Lots of love from all.

Your loving wife,

Jen.

Chapter 2

Love from Gallipoli

Shortly before her death in 1975, at the age of eighty-seven, Mrs Dorothy Slingsby donated to the Imperial War Museum seventeen letters written to her and her husband by Captain Ainslie Douglas Talbot, a regular army officer killed at Gallipoli in June 1915, as 'tokens of the personality and experiences of one very dear to me.'

Her late husband, Lieutenant-Colonel Tom Slingsby, MC, had been Talbot's closest friend while serving with the Lancashire Fusiliers in India before the war. And it was through him that Slingsby had corresponded with, met and later married Dorothy, the pretty army nurse Talbot would himself have married had he survived.

Tom and Dorothy married in 1918. But for sixty years Mrs Slingsby cherished the memory of the shy, handsome officer who had poured out his heart to her from one of the war's bloodiest battlefields.

'It was Douglas my mother was always in love with,' says Mrs Katharine Cleasby-Thompson, second of three daughters, who had cared for her after Colonel Slingsby's death. 'I think she was never in love with my father, though they got on very well together.

'Not long before her death mother asked me to read to her those old letters from Douglas. She was stricken with shingles,

35

in great pain and almost blind. She was coming to her end and I wanted to help her to look back – back to the personality she had been when she was young and in love. Sitting by a glowing December hearth, she listened intently, deeply moved, living it all again.'

Historically Talbot's letters are valued for the descriptions they give of the first landings on the Gallipoli beaches, on 25 April 1915, under a deadly concentration of Turkish machine gun and rifle fire, of which the Commander-in-Chief of the expedition, General Sir Ian Hamilton, wrote in an official dispatch: 'It is my firm conviction that no finer feat of arms has ever been achieved by the British soldier – or any other soldier.'

As love letters they are unusually touching, suggesting an emotional immaturity at odds with the sang-froid of a man of action who could write to his friend on the eve of the hazardous landings, 'It is all going to be so toppingly original.' Talbot was twenty-seven when he was killed, 'Dorfie' twenty-six, but their friendship, dating from their teens, had been, according to Mrs Cleaby-Thompson, a platonic one ('an affair of the intellect and the heart, not the body'). It is not until death looms close amid the carnage of Gallipoli that Talbot unleashes a passionate longing for her: 'Oh! you simply have been haunting me lately . . .'.

The only son of Colonel J.T.Talbot (for some years assistant commandant at the Royal Military College, Sandhurst), Douglas Talbot was educated at the Hindhead School, Haslemere, where he was 'crammed' for Sandhurst in his final year by Edward Turle, Dorothy's uncle. It was through him that he first met her, and her elder sister Mary, recently returned from Florence, where they had been enriching their restricted Edwardian education.

'From what my mother told me, Douglas's friendship was initially with her more beautiful, but less sympathetic sister Mary,' Mrs Cleasby-Thompson recalls. 'He made many visits to their home at Swanage in Dorset, where their father was a *general practitioner. But it was Dorothy he fell in love with. They found a mutual pleasure in their readings of poetry and the classics. Swanage was the scene of their greatest happiness – walking along the shore and the Purbeck Hills, picnicing beside a stream where she would sketch while Douglas fished.'*

Hints of an idyll reminiscent of Thomas Hardy and his Emma on the cliffs and strands of North Cornwall shine through the conventional verbiage of two poems Talbot wrote years later and sent to her – 'Studland Bay' and 'Dorothy'.

> *Sweet Bay of Studland, patron of my lay,*
>   *May thy propitious muse my song promote;*
> *Close to thy waters she and I did stray,*
>   *And there converse on worlds so far remote. . . .*
>
> *Dorothy, Dorothy. Maiden of mystery,*
> *Would I were with you as one time before,*
> *Living those moments of exquisite Bliss to me,*
> *Watching the waves on the surf-beaten shore. . . .*

The one bone of contention between Douglas and Dorothy was that he was a keen sportsman, she ardently opposed to blood-sports. Ironically it was this passion for hunting and shooting that cemented the friendship between Talbot and Slingsby when their regiment was posted to India in 1908. The gamebook they kept together has survived, a massive tome detailing the 'bags' on numerous shared expeditions on the trail of anything from tiger to waterfowl.

From tributes paid by fellow officers after his death, Talbot can be seen as a man with intellectual and artistic leanings who none the less threw himself wholeheartedly into the life of the regiment in its role as custodians of the British Raj, accepting its tradition-bound customs and taboos, and growing to prize that esprit de corps *that was to be so savagely tested at Gallipoli.*

'He was my subaltern for some time, and, although he was only a lad, I felt very much drawn to him for his cheery good nature,' a former commanding officer wrote to his parents. 'He was hard-working and conscientious and as a sportsman unparalleled. His love of nature was deep and thorough and when I got to know him better I was charmed with his great appreciation of beauty in nature and literature. You must have been very proud of such a son for he had a delightful nature when one got behind a certain reserve and shyness, and his ideas on things were delightful.'

A brother officer wrote: 'Douglas was a great admirer of good poetry, particularly of Lindsay Gordon. He taught me a great deal. He was one of the keenest naturalists I have ever come across. Many a time he and I have stalked up the edge of a jheel armed with field glasses and studied the habits of the many varieties of duck. Many a time, too, we have sat down on some ridge with our glasses and watched the glorious colourings of the distant snows of the Himalayas as the sun was setting.'

Talbot's first war letter to Dorothy was written from Karachi on 10 September 1914 shortly before his regiment embarked for England. Signing himself 'ever your loving friend', he thanks her for the bulky volume of Francis Thomson's poems she had sent him, alludes to the 'doubts and dreams' of some lines of Browning she has quoted, and hopes that 'you don't go as a nurse in a Hospital Ship, as I would not trust a German cruiser not to sink her if she got a chance.'

It was evidently in rebellion against her somewhat puritanical home background that Dorothy had signed on to train as a nurse at Charing Cross Hospital before the war. She had now completed her training, moved to a hospital in Nottingham and was contemplating enlisting as an army nurse. They had corresponded throughout Talbot's years in India and, on his return to England for training in September 1914, their renewed relationship was (according to what Mrs Cleasby-Thompson learned from her mother) 'blissfully happy'.

38

Talbot, who had specialised as a signals officer, was sta-
tioned at Nuneaton, of which he writes to Slingsby (who was
training with another battalion at Hull): 'Our men are having
the time of their lives in the billets, the whole place swarms with
very pretty factory girls – I should think that in 9 months' time
there should be the makings of a new Army in Nuneaton alone.'

Of chief interest in Talbot's letters to Slingsby, written before
he embarked for Gallipoli, are his references to the girl his
friend had not yet met but one day would marry:

. . . No! I am not engaged (legally as Mr J. would say), I
am waiting till I become a Captain. I will tell you about it
when I see you: of course between ourselves I am practically hooked, but I think it is better dark at present . . .

. . . Her ladyship has heard of you at times and I told her
you were dragging up to your fox, so to speak, she says she
hopes you will be as happy as we are, but she thinks that
could not be possible. I had a yarn from her great girl pal
the other day whose people apparently own a house and
forest in Scotland; so she may prove useful later on; as
Dorothy says I shall be able to stalk their deer and shoot
their grouse for them . . .

. . . Well enough now as I suppose I must send her
ladyship her daily letter. She is at Rotterdam at present
taking a rest after her strenuous days (with me) and is
staying with her sister, who is married to the Consul bloke
out there. . . . Her ladyship is going as Army Nurse now
instead of Navy. I tell her she's not going to nurse me!

. . . Yes, I shall soon be a Captain now as well as a
husband. Her ladyship is at Rotterdam. She says she is
longing to meet you. I have had several letters from her girl
pals, so in return you might write her one telling her what a

mug she is to care for me . . . Do write her a line, she will be so pleased and it does not matter what you say as long as you don't run me down too much . . . PS You are not to talk to her ladyship of me as 'the brat', or she will most likely let you have the rough side of her tongue, if she should have such a thing.

Talbot's next letter to Slingsby is dated 20 April 1915, five days before the landings:

I am afraid you will have to go on wondering where I am just yet, but you will most likely know before you get this. We expect a hell of a time here soon, I think there will be a surprise for most at home. I have to censor this myself and cannot tell you any news, I only wish I could . . .

Her ladyship is not bored with your writing – she was very bucked, especially with your second letter. I wish you were out here. It is all going to be so toppingly original. It is awful having to think hard whether you can say things before you put them down. At any rate we will have a good buck after the war if Doug lives. If I do get the knock you might drop a line to my sister Mrs Montgomery Millhuen [address given] as I should like you to be a pal of hers.

I shall be glad when we get 'up and at 'em'. At least I think I shall, 'poor deluded creature'. There is a devil on board who has been practising the charge on his bugle all the morning. The blokes over the way play 'Buy a Broom' as reveille, needless to say they are irregulars, but it sounds d–d well. Best love old flick,

Yours to serve, Addy

The Gallipoli campaign, aimed at forcing the Dardanelles,

capturing Constantinople and opening a back door into Germany, has variously been described as an unmitigated disaster, ineptly planned and executed, and an inspired enterprise that came near to hastening victory. What is incontestible is the gallantry of the officers and men picked to storm the beaches shortly after sunrise that Sunday morning of 25 April.

Spearhead of the British assault (while an Australian force landed some twelve miles to the north) was the 86th Infantry Brigade, comprising the 1st Lancashire Fusiliers, 2nd Royal Fusiliers, 1st Royal Munster Fusiliers, and 1st Dublin Fusiliers. With a proud tally of battle honours in far-flung corners of the Empire, and an esprit de corps second to none, they regarded themselves with some justification as an elite of the British regular army.

The elan with which they went into battle that doomed day had been fanned by a clarion call from their commanding officer, Brigadier-General Steuart Hare: 'FUSILIERS! Our Brigade is to have the honour to be the first to land and to cover the disembarkment of the Division. Our task will be no easy one. Let us carry it through in a way worthy of the traditions of the distinguished regiments of which the Fusilier Brigade is composed, in such a way that the men of Albuera and Minden, of Delhi and Lucknow, may hail us as their equals in valour and military achievement, and that future historians may say of us as Napier said of the Fusilier Brigade at Albuera: "Nothing could stop that astonishing infantry."'

The plan was to storm ashore, in the wake of a naval bombardment, at five simultaneous landing places around Cape Helles at the southern end of the peninsula. The Lancashire Fusiliers' objective was 'W' beach, a strip of powdery sand 350 yards wide and up to 40 yards deep, with low cliffs each side and sand dunes in the centre.

What no one had foreseen was the resistance that would be put up. A memorandum issued to the troops on the eve of the landings had dismissed the Turkish soldier as 'of very little use'.

41

As Talbot relates, the Fusiliers approached the beach laughing and joking, only to be met with a deadly accurate fusillade of machine-gun and sniper bullets, kept up for most of that day and night. 'The dead and wounded lay everywhere on the strip of sand and the sea for fifty yards out was streaked with blood,' wrote an eye-witness.

Talbot's descriptions of the landing were written some days later from a hospital ship lying off the beaches to which he had been taken, to his great chagrin, with a badly twisted ankle. His first note to Dorothy, dated 30 April, is merely to let her know he is alive:

Just a line, Dorfie darling, to let you know I am all strong. All correspondence has been stopped to and from here and this may never reach you; I am getting a wounded officer to post it at [censored] where he is shortly being sent. I have a strained ankle at present but expect to be back in the firing line soon. I did it falling into a trench on the second night. I do wonder what came out in the papers about this show at home.

Well girly thanks to your prayers etc. I have been most frightfully lucky so far. I long to talk about it all but musn't. Keep up cheer, mind. I know you must be awfully anxious, but worrying won't help either of us, and as I have escaped so far I should be able to escape anything I think. Best love and hope this reaches you fairly soon. I must say I just can't realise that my pals, who have already been killed, are dead. I find myself quoting 'Cathcuts Hill' to myself.

Your loving Douglas

5 May. On Board SS *Alaunia*.

Dear old Wang, [nickname for Slingsby]

I got through the landing without a scratch thanks to my

42

natural instinct to see cover on a flat beach, but sprained my ankle badly the second night falling into a trench in the dark. By jove it was pretty hot that Sunday morning. I can hardly write about it yet. Poor old Porter was killed by a hand grenade I think climbing up the cliff on my right. I am awfully sick he got knocked over. Tom Mansell and Tommy were shot getting out of the boat. I tell you I looked pretty slippy about getting ashore. I jumped overboard into 5 feet of water. I don't think the men realised how hot the fire was, they were laughing and joking till the last.

Well, I think we fairly made a name for ourselves as we were the first to establish a hold on the peninsula. I only got about five men ashore alive in my boat and not one of them could use their rifles owing to sand jamming the bolt. Bishop is d'd good and as cool as a cucumber under fire. Seeckham did d'd well all day. I believe he has since been hit through the shoulder. The sniping is simply awful here, one is more likely to get a bullet in the back than in the front. They hide all over the place. I don't think for the first 24 hours there was a single second when you could not hear a bullet overhead.

I must say I think this kind of fighting is a bit too warm for words. I had two horse gunner signallers with me the first day, who were with L battery in France, and they said they had never seen anything like that first landing. We spent the night on HMS *Euryalus* and landed in boats in tows early at daylight. I can tell you the sight of the peninsula being shelled by the fleet was grand with the sun rising above it all. We kicked off right outside the supporting ships and went in fairly fast until we were right under the cannon's mouth. The noise of the 10″ etc. were deafening.

We never got a shot fired at us till the oars were tossed around and then they started in earnest. The first bullet that struck the mate brought up loud jeers from our men, but poor devils they little thought what they were in for. Brockbank the runner was in my boat, he has a charmed life as he left his rifle on board and ran back for it and never got touched. C.S. Wilson was about the first man I saw hit, he got out first from the boat next me and was hit in the stomach at once. I didn't need Kipling's words to stop me from looking twice at him. Gus was hit just through the head above his eyes. I hope he won't lose his eyesight. Meakins was hit – his arm badly shattered, I am afraid he will have lost it. Kealy had his arm broken.

I don't know how much I am allowed to tell you of all this, but by the time you get this you will most likely know all the casualties. I must say I am sorry for the girls in Nuneaton, if they really cared: but it will show that part of the country what a soldier does have to go through.

Well, I expect to be back in the firing line in a day or so but my foot is still bruised and, although I feel an awful scrimshanker on this ship when I can see the battle going on on land, I know if I go too soon my foot will go again. I could not move my toes for the first day and Pirie thought it was broken.

Well best luck old chap. Do try and cheer my poor girl up. I am afraid when she finds out what the fighting is like out here it will make her feel rather sick.

Ever yours, Addy

2 May. It's no good, Dorfie, I've tried to write for half an hour but I simply can't. This is just to say I am well. I sent a letter by a wounded officer but in case you do not get it I came through the landing without a scratch. . . .

If you look in my gamebook you will see that the last two companions of my last shoot at Merivale were Porter and Thomas. They have both been killed. Porter was a good pal of mine. I often used to try to get him to write to you. He was also a very good shot and a topping sportsman and companion. I must say I simply can't believe that any of the regiment are dead yet.

Personally I lost no time in getting ashore and taking what little cover there was, though my boat got knocked out except about four, and the sand jammed their rifles so we had to lie still without being able to fire back and trust to not being hit. This was maddening, with a machine gun firing at us from under 150 yards.

However, thanks to providence I got out alright. This world doesn't seem right somehow, the next scene that comes to mind was a trench full of frightfully wounded men groaning and dying and a lark singing overhead as if it's heart was going to break with joy.

Waking or asleep, thou of death doth dream,
Things more true and deep than we mortals dream.

No I haven't got it right! But it struck me very forcibly at the time.

I'm afraid I'm getting most awfully callous. I don't think anything of the most awful sights now. I was having breakfast in the hospital tent the other day and a man went by with a leg in his hand, which had just been amputated, without chloroform. Poor devil, I have never heard such a row before. You, a nurse, can imagine what it is like out here. And here am I, who a fortnight ago would have got quite faint at a First Aid lecture looking upon it unmoved.

I find that actually in the show it's like a bad dream, you don't realise that you are alive hardly; it is afterwards when one starts to think of the numbers who have gone down that it upsets you a bit. I don't know how much information I may give, but as I have not told you of casualties except just 2 or 3 of us, I don't suppose it will get censored. We all wonder so much how much has appeared in the English papers and goodness knows what will be on or have

45

happened by the time you get this.

Don't worry about me, Dorfie darling, if I could get through the first Sunday without a scratch I feel there is something uncanny about it all, but don't think that that thought may lead to any more risks, as I shall take plenty of care of myself you may be sure as soon as I get in the firing line again. Our brigade did apparently very well indeed, I suppose it was quite a unique case in history, and the regiment did exceptionally in that they were the first to establish a hold on the peninsula, in spite of their losses.

Well, goodbye, girly, take care of yourself. I saw two nurses on a hospital ship yesterday, and they made me think of you so much. God blesss you and I hope in the end I may return safe and sound, but I am afraid it will be a very long way off yet-a-while.

Best love dear heart,

ever your own, Douglas

14 May. SS *Alaunia*. I think this is about the fifth time I have sat down and tried to write a letter to you, Dorfie darling. Like Bruce and the spider, isn't it? So let's hope I shall be successful this time.

I think I told you that I had not been able to get any letters since I left the firing line, goodness knows where they have got to. I have read your last batch over and over again in my bunk at night. Yes, I am glad you told your old soldier about me and of course I must be introduced to him when I come home. We will make a journey to the church that acted for your Hollow Tree and there we will thank God together for our safe reunion, if He so wills it.

Dorfie, you say in the photo I am more than a boy. What did you expect? Would you have a boy who is nothing else, ever, come out to face times like these? Boys were not allowed to come out with the Division, thank God. They knew what it was going to be like. Thank God I can be more than a boy sometimes, girl. And I can always return to my boyhood for your benefit. In fact, that is one of the brightest spots in our love, Dorfie, that when we are together we can forget the hard world and both be irresponsible kids again.

Yes, darling, your moods are rather wonderful, you led me to understand that when I nearly failed to make you come to Camberley* that it was because you thought I only loved you as a boy. You said you wanted strength to lean against, if need be, and then, when I put on a try to a man's expression in my photo you say the fact had practically broken down your ideals. Never mind, I understand how you feel, dear heart. And, as you say, nothing can come between us now.

Oh Dorfie! And does the fact that I exist make you straighten your back and keep your head. Oh! would that I were worthy for you to say such a thing. And here I am still with a crocked ankle when my brother officers are in the firing line. And yet if I go back too soon, as the doctor says, the thing will only go again and take twice as long to heal next time. And all this time I suppose you are picturing me at the head of my men leading the rush on the Turk trenches. I am afraid I should have very few of my original lot to follow now.

Oh! you simply have been haunting me lately. I have really been able to picture you. I suppose it is these times our souls yearn more than ever for communion. I see you now in your dear grey dress, now in the town kit, with the fur round your neck, leaning against the mantel at Inverness Terrace and saying: 'I want to be kissed by you!' What a fool I was. You would not have to wait long now. No. Don't blush. No one shall read this letter as I shall censor it

* His parents home.

47

myself. You bear witness that what I have said will not help the Turks.

Dorfie, when will, and what will, be the end of all this? Life is desperately hard, you are right. How many people have lived and loved in such hard times as these now present. Somehow the war is bearing me up. That go of malaria took all my bodily and mental strength away – if it had not been for your existence I should have longed to die. Now I know how sweet life can be. I have seen death all round me and although it is very beautiful and the more you see the more you believe in the future I simply long for the day when the cloud shall lift and we shall be together again in peace.

This place makes me think of the True Cross. How fitting that we should be fighting now so near where the Trojan warriors fought of old. Are they still asleep, Dorfie? When Queen Bess's guns go off do they raise a bony head and listen to the roar of the battle, smile, and sleep again? Can't you imagine them saying, 'At it again'. And then, what a fitting resting place for our 'Noble dead', beside Achilles and all the rest of old.

We've got 86 men all together in one grave just where we landed and as many again dotted over the hillside. Some day, when the war is over and we're sitting together on some grassy knoll, I may be able to tell you, with tears of pride in my eyes, of what happened. They are starting now, at the very thought of it. Oh Dorfie, the British regular Tommy is a marvellous fellow, to see him hurl himself to death with a smile on his face and a cheer on his lips. How I wish I could say the same of his Territorial brother. That is where *esprit de corps* and discipline comes in. But some day I will tell you all about it.

We are just beginning to get the English papers with accounts of the show out here. Poor little girl, you must have felt anxious. But cheer up, all is coming right. One thing I promise and that is, if I am taken, if it is possible for me to be near you and help you down here I shall do so as soon as possible. If not, I shall be waiting above and you must be patient.

Well, best love dear heart. And I hope I have not written too sad a letter but I can't bring myself to be so profane as to speak of this show as if I did not care a rap.

Ever your own, Douglas

Back on the peninsula, Talbot knuckled down to the stalemate of trench warfare that persisted for much of the eight months of the campaign, which ended with the surreptitious withdrawal of 115,000 men from under the noses of the Turks – the only operation that went triumphantly to plan. Total Allied casualties were estimated at 265,000, of whom some 46,000 were killed in action or died of wounds or sickness.

18 May. I have just got your letter from Uncle Ted, Dorfie. You need not try your flippancy by telling me not to be conceited. I know what an exalted idea your uncle has of me but I also know that he is quite wrong to say such things, and so they have no effect on my conceit.

This is the 18th or 19th I don't know which. We are attached to the Indian Brigade now and have been having a quiet time lately. Now we are within 400 yards of the enemy and have shots and shells over our heads day and night. We are in a position where we are supposed to be safe and we get a chance to bathe in the sea too. We expect to be in the trench itself in a day or so.

Dorfie, 'mylady', need not be frightened of vexing 'M'Lud' any more now as to the address as the latter is now a full blown captain. Perhaps you did not see it in the *Gazetteer*. Fancy, this time last year I did not expect it for

49

another 5 or 6 years.

How I wish we could go to Scotland for a week at once, Dorfie. This life is a bit too exciting in ways. My battalion has about 7 officers killed and 11 wounded so far. So your prayers are not in vain. We had a service last Sunday to the accompaniment of the screams of the shells and crack of the bullets. Do you know the 90th Psalm and the verse 'One thousand shall fall beside thee and ten thousand at thy right hand, but it shall not come nigh thee.' How true that verse has been. But we have lost far far finer men and officers than your Douglas.

As I write this there are shells bursting within 50 yards of my head but I am safe and always will be if God knows that your prayers are for what will be right. Dorfie, if I am taken. Don't be silly. Let the naval fellow have his deserts. Remember what Christ said of the women who had 7 husbands.

Just heard there is another mail on its way here. I wonder what you have heard of this. Don't be too anxious, it is not right Dorfie. The reason why your last budget was so long turning up was that they went to Alexandria in the wounded bag. I was going through the killed bag yesterday. They all have to be marked 'killed' and signed by an officer before being returned.

Dorfie, I was very very sad. I never realised who had gone before. Oh! this is an awful pencil and my fountain pen is dry. Like an ass I went for a swim in my watch yesterday and it is also *hors de combat*. Another of my pals has died of wounds. He was sent to the German Military Hospital at Alexandria with a shattered arm and they managed to give him gangrene. I believe it is an English staff there, but you need not worry, I shall refuse to go there if I am hit, if I get the chance. Now goodbye and good luck,

Your own Douglas.

Let my mother know my news. I have no time for more.

24 May. This is a bit of paper Mrs Bourne enclosed in a letter last mail, so you have her to thank for this. I don't suppose she put it in for this purpose though, so please write and tell her as I only had the bit of paper I used it to write to you on.

You wonder what I felt like that first landing. Not too bad really. And you say it would be good to see what I was doing sometimes. I thank God though that sometimes, at any rate, you can't do that. I know you can imagine what war must be like more or less as you see all the wounded etc., but there are far worse things than a freshly charred up man. Oh! it is all very well to talk of honour and glory but there is another side to war.

This place is nothing but a mass of dead KOSB's [King's Own Scottish Borderers] and Turks which fell on the 28th, are still unburied and the sun makes them very unbearable. I should think we will have disease shortly as the flies are getting awful. You say, why not bury the bodies. They are on the enemy's side of our parapet and if you put up a stick it is hit at once so it is impossible, you see our trenches now are only 150' away from the Turks. So there is no such thing as looking over the parapet, by day at any rate.

Two of our men did go out to bury one fellow who was more objectionable than the rest and in spite of several issues of rum they have been sick ever since. But enough, no more. Little do the civilians of England realise what war is. And the worst part is neither the Turks, or us, want to fight each other. Only the d'd Germans, who force them forward at the mouth of their own machine guns, I believe.

No, girl, I did not know I was a captain till a few days ago and even promotion now fails to thrill me. I would far sooner be with you in a cottage than be a Commander in Chief. Yes, I am still very keen. But such slaughter as is going on these days seems to be wrong, absolutely, to me. Why must we throw so many noble lives away as if they were dirt?

Well, cheer up. I am quite fit and cheery, really. But the stench around this place is beginning to get on my nerves: the more I see of war though, dear heart, and the sights I have seen of human remains have made me all the more certain that this life, where souls have to live in such bodies, is only a part of a training for the great hereafter.

How can any man think that a corpse is all that remains when a noble life goes out down here? Oh! I feel it all helps to show me how little this life really means. Well, we are all looking forward to the time it will be over. However much a small show may appeal to a man I don't believe anyone could say he liked a thing like this.

Best love dear heart. I hardly ever get a moment to look at your photo now and your last letter was read under a hail of shells and bullets, but safe in the trench, so don't worry.

Your boy, Douglas

27 May. Only a scrawl to say I am all OK I am at present with the 8th Manchesters, attached to them to give them advice.

I am quite cheery, Dorfy girl, so don't worry. Three of us spent the night at Divisional H'quarters the other night and they all drunk our health and the General said our landing was one of the finest deeds that had ever been performed, far far finer than Quebec. In fact they treated us like heroes. He said every man should have a VC if they had their rights. What now?*

* In the presence of so much heroism, six Victoria Crosses were allocated to the Lancashire fusiliers from which to make their own choice of recipients: two captains, two sergeants, a corporal and a private were chosen.

52

Please explain to my people how little chance I get to write, and paper and more especially envelopes are simply not to be got for love or money.

We are still in the clothes we landed in and have not had anything except what we actually carried ashore on our backs.

Best love, darling girl. I sometimes feel these days as if I simply daren't think of you or anything sentimental, with such awful realities to face. But I can't help it.

Ever your own, Douglas

30 May

My dear Wang,

Paper is very scarce these days but you can have this bit I think. You say Gallipoli sounds a bloody place. In ways, certainly. The whole place reeks of dead and yet it is a mass of flowers and would be quite divine without the war.

No. Don't you come out here. I feel sure France is much safer and I don't want you to double the chances of a future shooting being a wash-out. At present I don't feel like shooting anything except a German. Time after time I have been speaking to a man or standing next to him and he has dropped like a log. It is too damnable and by Jove these Turks can shoot too.

I was spotting with my own telescope today and it was d'd interesting. You could see the smiles on the Turks' faces as they were at the same game as us. They d'd nearly broke the lens of my telescope twice as they got half a dozen more to chime in. We had to climb down as I could not watch all of their rifles at the same time. My bloke bagged one though.

I am at present with the 8th Manchesters (to advise). They are a d'd good lot and did an advance yesterday any

53

regular battalion might be proud of. They are rather apt to get the jump as a body though, the men I mean. There is one chap called Captain Blenheim and I have never seen a cooler card. They had three officers killed and two wounded yesterday and 46 men killed or wounded. It is a wonder how many men are dropped dead in this blooming trench warfare. Practically all. By Jove I have had some luck so far.

Isn't it a bit too thick – going sick with a sprained ankle is bad enough, but the damned fools put me down as wounded although I did not appear in the papers. It is too rough on her ladyship: as a matter of fact I had two little cuts on my hand from a splintered bullet that needed dressing but I never thought they had got me down for a wound – it is too bloody.

Love and luck, Yours Addy

Talbot's last letter to Dorothy was written two days before he was killed during a general attack along the whole British front, launched in yet another attempt to push the Turkish lines farther back from the beaches. It was a day of stifling heat, a day clouded by dust and by the swarms of bloated flies that settled alike on the living and the dead.

Known as the Third Battle of Krithia, the attack was launched at noon, when a barrage from British battleships lifted and the troops sprang from their trenches to advance over no-man's-land with fixed bayonets. Within half an hour the Manchester Brigade, to which Talbot was attached, had overrun the enemy's front-line trenches and taken the second line, some 500 yards farther on. But later in the day, despite similarly heroic advances elsewhere, a withering enfilading fire forced a retirement. The gains, occupation of a central section of the Turkish front line trenches, had been negligible: the losses appalling.

According to a brief report sent to his parents by a Lancashire Fusiliers' officer, Talbot was accompanying the Colonel of the 8th Manchesters during the afternoon up a nullah, *or dried up watercourse, towards a Turkish position, when a shell exploded, killing both. The officer wrote: 'I can tell you definitely this – that he was perfectly happy up to the time of his death, not the least perturbed by the heavy fighting, and that his death was instantaneous.'*

Talbot's last letter was the third he had written in pencil to Dorothy on small sheets of a waterproof notebook, on which very slight seawater stains still show from the dowsing it got during the landing. One can only speculate as to how many more letters he might have written from the trenches, and how much more he might have let himself go, had it not been for the most mundane of reasons: an acute shortage of paper and envelopes.

2 June

My own little girl,

So you have been made most damnably anxious about your boy being wounded, it is too thick; it was bad enough to bear, having to go sick with my ankle, but to be made a laughing stock by being reported wounded, and make you so anxious, that is too much.

As a matter of fact I suppose they put the cut on my hand (which now I hear was caused by a splinter of a bullet which hit the belt of the man next me when we landed) down as a wound as it did fester a bit and I had to get a couple of stitches put in it on the ship. But as a wound it was nothing at all, and I never thought for a second they would report it.

It is rather warm here now for home kit and caps – they took our helmets off before we landed – but it is still cold at night.

How I wish I could see your dear face again but if God spares me like he has done to date I will: I must say I have had some marvellous escapes, ever since we landed, of course in that landing I don't know how anyone got through. I see they are putting a little detail in the papers now. We were the first ashore on beach W, and as you may gather from what it says in the papers we did put a different complexion on the affair, it is good to know we did such timely work as I don't suppose I better say more.

But enough! 'Heart of my heart let us talk of love.' I wish I had my Kipling or Lindsay Gordon here. You must get the latter if I don't come back. I love his character so. They are travelling about in my valise somewhere, we only have the kit we landed in.

You talk about being proud I am a Captain, Dorfie, but I did expect rather to hear of your pride of the doings of the regiment; it literally makes tears of pride come to my eyes whenever I think of what we have done; everyone says there is not a finer tale in history. You needn't be proud of me, I was only one drop in the ocean and was swept along on the tide of *esprit de corps*. I couldn't possibly have done the little I did single-handed. There are very few of the old 86th Brigade left.

How much would I give for a shady lawn, a comfy chair, and you in a hammock beside me; free as a bird in the air; at times this war seems to be going to be more than I can bear, but I know I really can bear much more, knowing what I have behind me, our love. I picture you in the grey army kit, walking along with your hands behind your back; I have often done so before, when I had fever at Karachi, I think I told you that there was a nurse there who reminded me very much of you, at least she seemed to be like you to my fevered brain; and the touch of her cool hand on my brow was yours entirely, so don't be jealous.

Please let my mother know you have heard as paper is

56

frightfully scarce, and I have had to think very carefully before I made up my mind to spare two sheets. Please ask my mother, too, to send me one of Steward's waterproof notebooks, as this one is nearly finished. They are wonderful books. This one has been swamped with sea water (on landing) but you would not know, would you?

Do give my love to Uncle Ted when next you write and explain that my correspondence is limited. Yes, as soon as we can after I get home, we will go and pay a good long visit together. I don't want any other place. Give my love to all the others, Mary Doris Dorothy and Co., and thank your mother for her letter.

Oh yes, Dorfie girl, won't it be topping to sit on a cool shady bank and watch the trout etc. Somehow I feel the sights I have seen in this war will make me a hundred times more humane in my sport; and yet sport does help you to understand war, as you say, but our love helps more than all these days.

God bless you girl,
Your Douglas boy

Attached to the letters of condolence to Talbot's parents from various officers in his regiment, there is one to Dorothy he would have prized as much as any – a tribute from one of those Tommy regulars he had seen in action and remembered with tears of pride. The letter is written from Malta, eighteen days after he was killed, and is signed A.H. Lewis-Hall (seemingly a medical officer).

Dear Miss Thurle,
Yesterday I was visiting one of the hospitals here – and there found a patient Singleton, 1st Lancs Fusiliers, and on hearing his Regiment I asked him if he knew Captain

Talbot and found that he had known him well. I was going to tell you of our conversation when I saw in the paper this morning that your fiancé had been killed. I am so very sorry. It is dreadful for you and he seems to have been so charming – Singleton was devoted to him.

Perhaps it will be some comfort to you to know how much his men liked him. Singleton told me that Captain Talbot sprained his ankle, was taken to a dressing station in the rear, but at first refused to go on a hospital ship and leave Gallipoli.

'He was that obstinate he didn't care what he did – but he wouldn't leave *us*. He was a nice officer – he'd do anything for *us* and we'd do anything for *him*. And him and me the best of chums tho' me only a private and him Captain. I was signaller – and a message came for Captain Talbot. I says, We 'aven't got no Captain Talbot, and then I gets the message that our Mr Talbot had been promoted. I *was* excited.

'And he was that brave – he didn't care what he did – always popping up to see what was going on. But wouldn't let us. Said it was too dangerous, but he did it himself. Oh, he was awfully brave – and he'd treat us all just like friends – have a game of football any time – and he was always laughing.'

Singleton was wounded in the battle on the 4th and knew nothing of Captain Talbot on that day. The casualties then were appalling. I've had the most harrowing shiploads of wounded. Of course his death is a terrible shock to you – but if you can only think that it is better for him to be killed at once instead of going through the terrible suffering that some have to bear – it may make it a little easier for you. This is a very depressing little island now. Wounded everywhere, the streets full of convalescents and the hospitals of terribly bad cases – and then funerals going past regularly twice a day. Luckily one can be kept busy – and I am sure

58

you are thankful to have your work now.

I told Singleton I should write and tell you what he'd said of Captain Talbot whom, yesterday, he hoped to see again in a few weeks – and as I was leaving the ward he called me back and said, 'Tell her he was always laughing.'

Dorothy believed that she knew the very instant when Douglas was killed. She was travelling on the top of a bus in Nottingham on the afternoon of 4 June when she was overwhelmed by a sudden foreboding. Grief stricken at his death, she joined the Queen Alexandra's Imperial Military Nursing Service, and got herself posted to Egypt, determined to see something of the Gallipoli peninsula for herself.

From what she later told her daughter Katharine, and from the eye-witness accounts of two officers of a woman seen on Cape Helles in November 1915, it seems clear that she actually managed to land on the peninsula, from a hospital ship, while the fighting was still in progress, but that she was turned back before finding her fiancé's grave.

While Dorothy was ministering to the tragic wrecks of Gallipoli in Egypt, and later on the hospital ship Lanfranc, *Tom Slingsby was making a regimental name for himself on the Western Front, being awarded the Military Cross during the Third Battle of Ypres in 1917. The bond that Douglas had forged between them was strengthened by mutual grief at his death. They married in 1918. The 2nd Battalion Lancashire Fusiliers were posted back to India, where the Singsby's joined them in 1927 and where their three daughters were born.*

'My father must have always been aware of mother's undying love for Douglas, though he never talked about him to us,' says Mrs Cleasby-Thompson. 'But there was great companionship in their marriage. Though his obsession for bloodsports went counter to her gentle nature, she came to terms with it. She learned to ride and made a jolly good effort in sharing

59

his sporting enthusiasms. Despite the differences in their back-grounds and temperament, they really got on very well together.'

Mrs Cleasby-Thompson is herself married to a Lancashire Fusiliers' officer. She married him immediately after the eva-cuation from Dunkirk in 1940, determined that, unlike her mother, she would have at least known the happiness of marriage should he later be killed. They live today in an army training area near Thetford in Norfolk, not far from the cottage where her mother spent the last years of her life as a widow. Displayed in the sitting-room are her mother's framed photo-graphs of Tom and Douglas. In regimental dress uniform they look remarkable alike, with identically flattened-down dark hair and neat moustaches.

'I was always very close to my mother,' says Mrs Cleasby-Thompson. 'Towards the end I shared with her as never before the memories she had put to one side, like the letters from Douglas, to lead her new life. As I read them aloud to her by her fireside, she was once again in memory walking with Douglas along the Swanage shore and on the hills, the wind in their hair. The end was peaceful. After the funeral service before the cremation, a winter wind was blowing storm clouds across the sky when we came out of the village church at Cress-ingham, and then the sun shone through and a perfect rainbow arched overhead.'

Shortly before she died Dorothy Slingsby confided to her daughter her last wish: that her ashes should be taken to Galli-poli and scattered on the beach where Douglas and his gallant comrades had made their historic landing. The ashes of Tom Slingsby had been scattered, at his request, around a fox covert in his favourite hunting country in Hertfordshire.

'Through a friend the Turkish Military Attaché was approached at the embassy in London with the idea that a small ceremony might mark the scattering of the ashes on "W" beach,' says Mrs Cleasby-Thompson. 'This was at the time of Crete, *Cyprus "*when Anglo-Turkish relations were strained, and it was sugges-

ted that such a ceremony might be in the nature of a rapproche-
ment. I put my mother's ashes in their urn at the bottom of her
grandfather clock to await a reply.

'Weeks went by, my friend repeated the request, but still we
heard nothing. When it seemed certain that nothing would tran-
spire, I took the ashes to a part of the countryside near here that
my mother had particularly loved and scattered them under an
oak tree. Just a week later we got a letter from the Turkish
Embassy apologising for the delay and warmly accepting the
idea of such a ceremony.

'I still feel very bitter about it – if only they had said they
were going into the request I would have waited. The important
thing is that she died, as she had lived, confident in the belief
that love outlives death, confident in the truth of those words
Douglas had written from Gallipoli, with a presentiment of his
own death: "I shall be waiting above and you must be
patient."'

Chapter 3

Tommy in the Trenches

By the summer of 1915 an awareness was growing on the home front that life in the trenches for the Tommy was not quite as depicted in flowery reports in the press, whimsical Punch cartoons, recruiting propoganda. Parcels of 'comforts' (knitwear, cigarettes, goodies) began to stream out to the Western Front, even from those with no husband, son or boy friend to be personally concerned about.

In a church hall in Walthamstow one June Sunday a Sunday School teacher called Ivy Williams asked her class if any of them had fathers in France who might like her to send a parcel. There was no response until a small boy piped up, 'My Dad ain't, Miss, but my Uncle Jack is.'

It was thus that Private Daniel John Sweeney of the 2nd Battalion, the Lincoln Regiment, received out of the blue a letter with a parcel that was to change the course of his life. The correspondence that followed led to his meeting Ivy on leave a year later. He fell in love with her. On a second leave the following year they became engaged. At the end of 1917 Sweeney was invalided home, and shortly afterwards they married.

Sweeney's voluminous letters would be of considerable interest, even without their touching love interest, as showing the reactions of a seasoned regular to three years of trench

63

warfare. After his death in 1961, indeed, Ivy Sweeney prepared an edited version of the letters for the interest of their children and grandchildren, omitting what she calls the 'lovey-dovey bits'. But she had no reservations about donating most of the original letters to the Imperial War Museum. They tell of a romance that not only survived a war but dissolved a class barrier.

Ivy came from what would then have been known as the lower-middle class, Jack from the working class. Ivy's father was managing clerk in a firm of solicitors, Jack's a confectioner. Ivy's home was a terrace house in the east London suburb of Walthamstow, Jack's a tenement flat in Clerkenwell. Ivy had been educated at a private school and technical college and was working as a solicitor's clerk. Jack had had a rudimentary council school education (as the spelling and grammar in his letters indicate) and had enlisted in the army at the age of eighteen. When the correspondence started Jack was twenty-seven, Ivy twenty-six.

Sweeney's early letters suggest some misgiving about the difference in their backgrounds. 'Please remember that I am not a CITY CLEARK, *don't laugh I am a Dunce' he wrote in one letter shortly before they were to meet for the first time. Ivy's letters have not survived to reveal her rejoinder. But looking back, at the age of eighty-seven, she recalls that she saw no reason for such self-deprecation. 'I found that Jack knew how to describe things far better than most educated people,' she says. 'He wrote from the heart.'*

Sweeney's boyhood had been an unhappy as well as a deprived one. His mother died when he was ten and his father remarried. His stepmother treated him badly and, at the age of fifteen, he ran away from home with a Romany travelling circus. His father, with whom he got on well, informed the police and he was eventually picked up in Dover. There is a letter from the superintendent of a Church of England mission there to his father asking if he should be sent back home. 'I trust

64

*you will take him back,' he writes 'as he seems truly sorry for the
sin he has committed. It would be a great pity to allow one so
young to go to the bad.'*

*What Sweeney did, after three more unhappy years at home,
was to join the army. Although discipline and training were
rigorous, his seven years' service with the 2nd Lincolns up to the
outbreak of war were the happiest of his life until then. In 1912
the battalion was posted to Gibraltar, and a year later to
Bermuda. It was from these idyllic islands that the battalion
returned to England to face the rigours of winter in the Flanders
trenches.*

*Sweeney's first letter from the front was to his father, dated
20 November 1914. (In subsequent extracts Sweeney's spelling
has been corrected as being needlessly distracting.)*

Well Dad I have been in the Trenches from last Friday
until Tuesday and would have enjoyed it very much only
for the Rain which made us look like Mudlarks. Well Dad
we have had a few narrow escapes, that was last Sunday,
the Germans sent us a few presents from the Kazar, they
were Shrapnell Shells or as we call them Jack Johnsons they
came verry near our trenches but never hurt anybody and
the boys was laughing every time one Bursted.

It is a pittyfull Sight to see some of the Towns hear all in
Ruines and No People about, the Churches are the
Germans aiming mark . . .

With love to you all I remain your loving son Jack

PS. We get a nice Drop of Rum every Day.

*By the time the correspondence with Ivy started eight months
later, Sweeney had spent a spell in hospital with a head wound
from a bullet and had seen enough of trench warfare to have*

65

begun envying those who had 'caught a Blighty one' (a wound serious enough to be sent home). During his years at the front he appears to have spent part of his time as officers' cook (in the trenches as well as at rest camps), part as infantryman. Often in the thick of the fighting, he was eventually one of the few survivors of the original battalion.

The letters, mostly scrawled in pencil and sometimes running to ten pages or more, show how much Sweeney came to depend on Ivy's replies to keep his spirits up. Apart from major offensives, like the Battle of the Somme in 1916 and the Third Battle of Ypres in 1917, which Ivy would be reading about in the newspapers, he gives little indication as to which sector of the front he is writing from. As in most accounts by Tommies, the war is seen as a blurred succession of active and inactive periods. Some of the grimmer experiences he records are at times when all was officially quiet on the Western Front.

The first parcel, with a letter written by Ivy, was sent communally by the Williams family, and Sweeney replies to 'My dear Friends' (thereafter he writes directly to Ivy). At the time he was on his way to the Ypres front, where massive bombardments and bitter fighting had been in progress since April, and the ancient town of Ypres had been reduced to rubble.

19 July 1915. I received your parcel on the same afternoon as I left Rouen to come to this place. The name of this place I am not allowed to tell you. It could not have come at a better time as we were in the train from 12 p.m. on Friday night until 9.15 a.m. on Sunday and all we had in the way of food was six hard biscuits and a pound of bully beef so you can see how nice that box of chocolates was to me and my chums.

We are now settled down here for about two weeks to learn the Maxim Gun then we have to go up to our Regiments which are at present in one of the worst parts of the firing line known to us men as 'Worse than Hell'. It is a terrible place and fighting is always going on there, you read a lot in the papers about the same place. It was once one of the prettiest towns in France, but now it is only a heap of ruins with dead civilians and soldiers everywhere, if only the slackers of England were to see this place I do not think they could hang back any longer, especially the little children and young women who have been killed there – but most of the people in England do not realise what a terrible war this is.

Even our soldiers dread to hear that they have got to go to this place – anywhere except there is the cry. I dread going myself, but of course someone must go so it is not any good going with a sad heart. I always say to myself if it is God's wish that I get wounded or killed it is to be and no one can stop it, but I do wish He would stop this murder.

Well dear Friends I am afraid you will think me a lively feller telling you this but I do like to speak my mind and not write and say things that happen and never do. I must say that the boys are always cheerful, it is surprising what a spirit an English soldier has, no matter if it is pouring with rain and they are wet to the skin they still keep singing, they sing all the more if it rains faster, it is a good job we have got men like that or else I do not know where we would be.

Well dear Friends I have not much more to tell you only this place is very pretty, it is a Convent a good way from the town and we do our drills in the grounds and sleep in tents now that it is hot. There are a lot of little girls in this Convent, such nice little mites some of them are, we only see them once a day and they all chatter, but I cannot understand much French – I wish I could.

Wishing you all the very best of health and luck,

I remain yours sincerely, Daniel John Sweeney. Good Night.

30 July. . . . I was very pleased that you liked my letter. I was wild with myself afterwards because I wrote such horrible stuff but it was quite true and perhaps it told you more than you had heard before in the papers.

Well you say my sister has promised you a photo of me. I have told her to give you one of myself and a friend of mine who was a sailor but went down in his boat somewhere in the Dardanelles. You must excuse this writing but I am in a very awkward place on the grass, we have no reading room or anywhere else where we can write so we have to do the best we can. . . .

17 August. . . . We are digging some trenches about 2 miles behind the firing line – I am with my old Captain who was in charge of our Machine Guns at the battle of Neuve Chapelle where he was wounded. I am his Orderly, he is a gentleman, not one of those who are always bullying their men and he gets a lot more work done by treating men as men. The weather out here is very hot and makes us so thirsty and we are allowed only so much water – if we have any other water than that which comes out of the Water Cart we have to boil it before drinking it owing to so much fever being about. We are going to win, but I cannot see any finishing to it just yet.

It was terrible last winter, I do not know how I managed to stick it without a day's illness, but I did. I saw strong men crying because their feet were so cold and frostbitten, we used to be up to our waist in water and mud for three days and nights without any sleep and very little to eat, we had the food but could not find any dry place to cook it. Most of the people at home round their big fires would not believe it. After we had had three days and nights in the trenches another regiment would come and relieve us, then we had three days rest and in that three days we had to dry and wash our clothes, get all the mud off then back to the trenches to get wet through again. It was FINE 'I don't think'. . . .

22 August. . . . Of course the Badge was meant for you why did you ask? Well I am at present sitting on the lawn in front of my officer's house and I have a big box which is layed out with your parcel and your letters. I know my officer won't wind because I have just let him sample my Butter Scotch and a stick of chocolate. He wanted to know if this letter was for my Fiancée. What cheek, he is always joking. . . .

Well Ivy you have made me quite frightened to come home, I must tell you I am a very shy young man when I am in the company of ladies so you had better keep a sharp eye on me in case I run away. I must be brave when that day comes so please be very careful and do not make too much fuss of me or perhaps I shall have to go into hospital with my nerves. . . .

25 September. . . . I had a young lady (only once) but when I went to Gibraltar she seemed to get tired of waiting so I have never troubled about girls since and I don't think I ever shall again, but I may be lucky one day and find a nice young lady who will have me, at least I hope so but I think last winter spoiled my looks and the Battle of Neuve Chapelle I am sure made me look 40 years older. . . .

12 October. . . . As I have told you I cook in the same room as the officers and they do have a game with me. The other night I was seeing to the soup and they were all around the stove and I could hardly move, I was putting some pepper into the soup when the Captain said 'Be a bit more liberal with the pepper' and knocked my hand and a lot more went into the pot than ought to have done, then at dinner he had

69

the cheek to say that there was too much pepper in the soup. They hide all my utensils and they enjoy it very much if I happen to burn myself and often try and make me burn myself, they are a lot of 'lads' always happy when in mischief. . . .

17 October. At last I have arrived at the fighting line and a terrible place it is, the very worst part of the line and there is always fighting going on here. It is the place I told you we call 'Worse than Hell'. Well dear I have not much time and never will have now to write you a nice letter. I am going into the trenches tonight and speaking truly I dread going but I expect someone has got to do it. . . .

All we can hear is, bang, bang, bang, it is shells everywhere. I am trusting to God to pull me through. Give my love to all,

I remain your loving friend Jack.

14 December. . . . We left this place 'Hell' as I call it six weeks ago and came to this place which is just like heaven compared to Ypres the place we were at. We are now in the trenches which are just in front of a very big town. When we are out of the trenches we go into billets in this town and we have had a few shells on our house. Last time we were out a shell came and caught 3 of our officers and 20 men – all wounded – one blown to pieces.

I expect you will hardly believe me when I tell you that the civilians are still in the town. We can go out and buy anything we want, that is if we have any money which we get very little of. All the public houses are open and the tea shops, jewellers shops as well, it is just like London. We could have a fine time here when we are out of the trenches if the 'Stingy Government' would give us a little more to spend. We get five francs every month, that is 4 shillings and twopence in English money, that does not last two hours here when a fellow buys a loaf of bread and a couple of eggs to take in the trenches with him it is nearly all gone.

There are some lovely Xmas presents here which I would like to send you but I can only see one way of getting them and that is if the Germans send a shell into the front window of the shop, then we may be able to borrow a few things until after the war. . . .

16 December. . . . Well Ivy you say that you pray for me every night, and I thank you for it. I know a lot of men here before the war were great sinners but I know that they often pray now, it is the time the Germans are shelling our trenches that they think there is a God. I am not saying that I said my prayers before the war because I did not but I don't believe I have missed a night since I have been out here and ever since the Battle of Neuve Chapelle I have believed there is a God because I prayed to Him before the battle to keep me safe and He did, I had some marvellous escapes. . . .

18 December. . . . I must again thank you for your lovely parcel, I am going to take the Cake into the trenches and keep it for Xmas Day tea time and fancy I am at home having tea, so think of me at 4.30 Xmas Day having a big Blow Out. . . .

9 January 1916. . . . I am very pleased you thought of me at 4.30 on Xmas Day – your cake then saw what the trenches was like but not for long as me and a few Chums soon put it in a good dug-out and it was very nice indeed. . . .

4 February. I cannot understand why I have not heard from you for so long, I hope that you are not ill. I have written to you 2 letters and I have not had any answer yet. Well Ivy

71

dear we have been having a most horrible time, the War is worse than ever it was (War I said, I mean Murder) it is cruel. I am almost done and candidly speaking I have often longed to be wounded to get away from this place for a little while.

It has been snowing very hard today and is very cold but that don't make any difference in the War. I do wish it was all over I have had quite enough of this life and my nerves are not of the best now, I cannot get to sleep and when I do I have the most horrible dreams, can you wonder at it. . . .

24 February. . . . I had just finished serving the officers dinner up and we were clearing the table when there was a crash – I did not run – I went into my dug-out with another man, this dug-out was a sheet of corrugated iron that is all. The officers were shouting 'stand to men', but we could not as we were buried – my God I thought my last moment had come, it was pitch dark and every shell that burst seemed like a flash of lightning – shells were bursting all round us.

We were quite helpless as we could not get out and to make it worse I could not see where the other man was. I shouted to him but he did not answer I thought he was killed, but he told me afterwards that he tried to answer me but could not speak. How long I was buried I do not know, however, the officers knew we were there and at last a party of men came and dug me out, also the other man whom I expected to see dead. We had 900 shells that night and the following afternoon were bombarded with another 400. . . .

2 March. . . . Well Ivy dear I am sure you would make a nice nurse in fact you are better than all the doctors as they don't seem to buck a lad up at all, but one of your letters is far better than all the pick-me-ups the doctor can give me. . . .

12 April. . . . We were bombarded for three hours and then a small party of Germans got into our trenches and all had bombs which they did a bit of damage with. We only caught one, he was a German officer and he stabbed one of our officers, and when the boys went to bayonet the German our officer stopped them and told them to have mercy on him, which they had to do much against their will. They also sent tear shells and gas which played us up a bit, it was a bad time and we lost a lot of men – buried by these cylinders. I had one of the closest shaves I have ever had, but I am safe although badly shaken. I am sure this war will send us all mad, people at home cannot realise what the lads out here go through. Anyway we do our best to keep happy. . . .

25 April. . . . I am sure Ivy that you are not one of those girls that think yourself high up in the World and I guess you can give and take a good joke. I think that you must be a very jolly girl to be with, one who makes any unhappy person forget their troubles, as for me I am the most miserable lad on earth sometimes – especially when I cannot get a smoke. I do hope you don't mind a boy having a smoke in your company, go on hit me. . . .

2 May. . . . Yes My Dear I know that I have never seen you but I am sure we will soon be able to see and meet each other, then I expect I shall be so shy. I know what I shall do when I knock at your door I shall put on my Gas Helmet then you will not be able to see me blushing (good idea). Yes My Dear I think it would be best for me to wait until I see you in life instead of having a photo, but all the same *I should like the photo please*. No Ivy Dear I shall try and not be shy and as you say you will soon make me feel at home but do please remember that I am not a city clerk, don't laugh I am a Dunce. . . .

73

16 May. Thank you very much for your splendid letter and photo which I have just received. I am so glad that you have sent me the photo, it is as you said in your letter but I think it is very good for a snapshot only the bushes at the back make it so dark. I wonder where those 2 Scotch soldiers are now, perhaps they are home wounded again or perhaps, only perhaps, they are 'pushing up the daisies' out here.

It is simply murder at this part of the line. There is one of our officers hanging on the Germans' barbed wire and a lot of attempts have been made to get him and a lot of brave men have lost their lives in the attempt. The Germans know that we are sure to try and get him in so all they do is put 2 or 3 fix rifles on to him and fire every few seconds. He must be riddled with bullets by now, he was leading a bombing party one night and got fixed in the wire – the raid was a failure.

The bombardments at this point are too awful to tell you, it is a wonder anybody is alive, and both sides are always blowing up mines, they do not give any warning all one knows is that there is a rumble like an earthquake then up goes anybody who happens to be in that part of the trench. . . .

A month later Sweeney was home on ten days' leave. When he knocked, with some trepidation, on the door of 7 Maude Terrace, Walthamstow, it was Ivy's mother, not Ivy, who answered.

'I got home from work a little later,' Mrs Sweeney recalls. 'I remember going into the living room saying "Any letter from the front?" turning round and a soldier was sitting in the corner. I said "Good gracious me, where have you come from!" He said "Are you Ivy?" I said "Yes, are you Jack?" He said "Yes."

'He was much quieter than I'd expected, gentle and with a lovely face. I'd told him all about another soldier I'd been going out with but had recently parted company from, and wasn't expecting anything special to come of our meeting. For him I think it was love at first sight. For me the real love came later.

'Jack was worried I was too educated for him, but I told him it didn't make any difference whatsoever. At first my father thought he was perhaps not good enough for me, but soon became as fond of him as my mother. Many years later it was Jack he asked for when he was dying.

'Those were very strict days and when I suggested we might go to a show one night Mother said "You'll have to get Dad to take you." So Dad took us to the Coliseum for a variety show. But we had walks together and I saw him off at Waterloo. I gave him a kiss, though I also gave a kiss to another soldier he was with.'

Ivy Sweeney's most treasured letter, withheld from those she donated to the Imperial War Museum, was sent by Jack on his return to the front:

I've reached my destination at 6 o'clock on Tuesday evening, and I feel so miserable but I'm trying to buck up now. Well Ivy dear I am so pleased that you managed to come to Waterloo to see me off. I had such a lot to tell you but could not when I saw you.

Dear Ivy I've fallen in love with you. Perhaps Ivy you will say why did I not tell you that, well because I was afraid dear I would have been doing wrong. I hope you will not be offended with me, I know you will not. I know if I cannot be your boy I will love you as a loving friend. I feel so unhappy at present but I expect I will be alright in a day or two. I have not much time to write more dear as I will be very busy.

Fondest love to Mother and Dad, best respects to Olive

and Charles [Ivy's sister and brother], fondest love to your-self.

Jack

What Sweeney was to be busy about for some time to come was the Battle of the Somme, launched on 1 July 1916. Rumours of a major Allied offensive, confidently expected to breach the German lines and end the war, had been circulating before Sweeney went on leave, and he had told Ivy what was in the air. Whether or not she had this in mind, her reply to his declaration of love was evidently warm enough to give him new heart for the hazards ahead.

23 June. I have just received your most welcome letter of the 16th June. I am in the trenches and I cannot tell you how happy it has made me as I must confess I have been downhearted just lately. . . . Well my Darling I am so glad that my letter did not offend you but I was silly not to have told you I loved you when I was with you but really I did not know if I might have offended you and then my dear little Ivy may have left me. But now I know and you have made me so happy I can fight out here now with a good heart knowing that I am fighting for such a Darling Girl.

Yes my dear Ivy I would love to be walking down Cannon Street now with you. I had a mind to tell you then but I expect that I was too shy, but never mind I shall know when I come home again what to say, but how much happier we could have been if I only knew before, but it was meant to be was it not. . . .

I close with my fondest love and thousands of kisses and remain your loving boy,

Jack

The Battle of the Somme, 1 July to 16 November, in which the British suffered over 400,000 casualties, nearly 60,000 of them on the first day, has been written about more than any other battle in the First World War. In Sweeney's lengthy, disjointed and breathless descriptions of the actions in which he took part (now transferred from the 2nd to the 1st battalion of the Lincoln Regiment), one gets some idea of what such carnage and chaos meant to the Poor Bloody Infantry.

A massive five-day bombardment had preceded the launching of the attack and for much of this time Sweeney had been under retaliatory shell-fire in the trenches. When his battalion was relieved on 29 June ('about done up as it was a terrible strain on anyone's nerves, no sleep and nothing else but shells day and night') it was in the expectation of a rest period.

. . . We left the trench and went into a dug-out about 2 miles behind the firing line and slept all day. On the 30th we cleaned up and had a wash and shave, the first wash for ten days. We then received orders that greatly surprised all of the boys, and this is what it was, the attack was going to be made on the 1st July, and we were in support. On our way up to the firing line every man had to carry something, some would have tools and water cans etc., I had to carry a box of four Stokes Shells which were no light weight.

Well the morning of the 1st came and I was very tired as we had not had much rest but it had to be done and no one knew even on the morning of the 1st what time the attack was being made but the artillery started at 6.30 a.m. and at 7.30 we heard the CO shout 'The boys are going over.' Where we were, by getting on the hill near us, we could see the boys going like mad across 'no-man's-land' but we could not look for long as Fritz's artillery observers might have spotted us.

At 8 o'clock we began to move up but we had to go very slowly up the communication trenches as Fritz was shelling all of them, we got our loads and after a very hot time we came into our own fire trench. Now was the worst part of the job as we had to get up the ladders and get across to the German trench as quickly as we could, how I managed it I shall never be able to tell, but as soon as we were all on top the Germans started sending big shrapnel shells – terrible things – I heard when we got into the German first line of trenches that 15 of our boys were killed and wounded coming across, and when we got into his first line we lost 24 men killed by one shell. I was blown against the back of the trench and just managed to get into a German dug-out before 3 more big ones came.

That night we had to go into the firing line and relieve the boys who had made the charge. We captured 4 lines of trenches that day – not so bad. We got into those trenches safely and after we had been there a few hours Fritz started his counter attack. We mowed them down in hundreds and they did not get within 20 yards of our trenches, they soon got fed up and did not try again that night.

We were in the firing line all the night of the 1st also the 2nd and we were relieved on the night of the 3rd. We all came out by way of a road and we were very lucky in not getting one wounded.

Well my Darling we are now out of hearing of the guns as we have had a 26 mile train ride, but I do not think it will be long before we are 'at them' again, but at present we are not strong enough. I told you Dear I was happy well so I am, but when I think of my poor dear old chums who have fallen I could cry. I had to cry in the trench about one of my chums poor old Jack Nokes, he has been out here since the beginning of the war and had not received a scratch, he has never been home on leave because of a small crime. Poor lad he died game with his mother's name his last word. I cried like a child, not only him but a lot more of my poor comrades have gone.

Ivy my Darling I am sure it is you and my poor sister praying for me that God has spared me. I said my prayers at least 1000 times a day (Please God spare me to get out of this war safely for my dear Ívy's and my sister's sake). O Ivy I cannot tell you the horrors of this war, you cannot realise what it is like to see poor lads lying about with such terrible wounds and we cannot help them.

We have come out of this action with 4 officers out of 26 and 435 men out of 1,150. I am glad to say that most of them are wounded and I can say that for every 1 of our dead there are 10 German dead. I have accounted for 14 as I am certain of but I believe I killed 12 in one dug-out – I gave them 8 bombs, one for 'Kitchener' and the others for my chums.

One German very nearly proved himself a better man than me and he might have had me if it had not been that two of our men came on the scene, we took him prisoner so he couldn't grumble ('Mercy Kamerad' is all that we can get out of them and 'English very good'). Well we took hundreds of prisoners that day and they were glad to be prisoners, but we made them work like slaves, we made them carry water and ammunition up to the firing line and some of them could not stand when we had finished with them. . . .

Part of the next letter Ivy received must have surprised, even shocked, her. It was written from a rest camp, during a temporary respite from the vicious fighting, and is a prime example of the macabre humour that was, from all accounts, the Tommy's safety-valve against the horrors surrounding him.

2 August. . . . Last Sunday 31st July it was a splendid day and ever so hot, we had the afternoon to ourselves there was a nice stream a little distance from our billet so me and my little friend the Corporal decided to go and have a swim so off we went.

Well dear our little Friends are very troublesome this weather and make a lot of attacks on us. We arrived at the stream and undressed and of course we had to have a look in our Friends' trenches (shirt seams) to try and find how strong our enemy was, and my word I must confess that in my trenches were not less than 1000.

Well we laid the shirts in the sun and had a bit of a swim which we enjoyed very much. When I went towards my shirt what do you think I saw? Why I saw such a big Battle on. I found that I had laid my shirt on an old ant hill and my shirt was covered with them, they were attacking my Bosom Friends. I must say that my side lost very heavily in fact I could not find any who had escaped. Well when I told the boys about this they all went with their shirts to join the battle. My word the ants beat all the Keatings and other powders as they are sure to find all the enemy, they know how to fetch them out of their dug-outs.

I was a bit comfortable for a day or two but after that my Bosom Friends found a new thing and now he is having his own back on me. But all is fair in love and war so we musn't grumble.

I say Ivy how would you like me to send a few, you could tame them it would be a fine hobby. I have all sizes and colours. You could let them loose in bed so as to have a feed. What do you think of me, please forgive me if I am rude but we must try and keep happy if it is only this way. . . .

This letter was written shortly after Sweeney had survived a nightmare experience in Mametz Wood, one of the key strongpoints on the Somme front. Like other woods in the German lines it was a labyrinth of trenches and dugouts which had to be fought for every inch of the way. Sweeney's confused account was written in retrospect, over three months after the event, evidently in reply to a query by Ivy about a soldier who had been killed in the action.

6 November. It was on the evening of the 18th or 20th of July (not sure of date) that I found the body of Pte Salway. I was sent with 30 men out of the firing line which was then in Mametz Wood. It was terrible fighting and the cries of the wounded were heart rending, we could not do anything for some of the poor lads but we managed to carry a few of them out with us. There were many dead of both sides but mostly German who I must say looked as though they had put up a good fight.

The wood was being shelled everywhere – we lost 7 men getting out, 4 were blown to pieces, I cannot describe what it was like but we wanted bombs and someone had to get them so I was one of the unlucky chaps who had to fetch them. It was a treat to get out of that hell for a couple of hours but it was getting out of it safely that was the trouble.

Well we got the bombs from the 'Dump' (as the Stores are called) and were on our way back in the dark in single file when all at once a shell burst just in front of us. Myself and 2 more men happened to be passing a trench so we dodged in there for safety, 2 more shells came so we went up this trench which led to another road and we expected to meet the other chaps at the cross-roads but could not find them.

Well we knew our road back but speaking the truth we were in no hurry to go back to that hell so we stopped at the next line of trenches and Fritz was shelling a place on our right so we decided to get into the trench running from a road known as The Sunken Road. Just at the corner of the trench we saw 2 men lying, one on one side of the road the other on the other side.

The moon was very bright, the man on the right was in a terrible state, his blood was draining from him into the middle of the road, his head (or all that was left of it) was covered with a sandbag, we did not touch him at all. The other man was covered with a sandbag but he was not hit about the body like the man opposite. Well something seemed to tell me to look in his pockets, he is the first dead man I have ever touched but I did it and I found a few photos of himself and his wife and children, a pipe and baccy and 1 franc and a ½.

Well we got a light and looked at his letters to see who he was, when I saw the address on the top of his letter (his home address) I could have dropped as I knew it very well and I believe I knew the man too. The letter was the last one from his wife and I kept it until after the battle and we got relieved. I left his Pay Book also his identification disc so as the burning party would know who he was, then we went on our journey with our box of bombs. . . .

After we were relieved we went by train to a place called Arras, I then sent that letter which I found on Pte Salway to his wife and she wrote back and thanked me and asked if I happened to find out where he was buried if I would let her know. Well when we left Arras to go to that 'Hell' again I had a look at a good many graves around the spot where I found Pte Salway but I did not find it.

I know where he must be buried now, it is in one of the big grave grounds, I passed it on the march. There are about 800 buried there, the graves are well looked after but some of the poor chaps are buried where they fell and a bit of wood made into a Cross to show that some poor lad is buried there, some have no names, others bear on them 'An Unknown English Soldier'.

In Mametz Wood there are not hundreds of dead but I should say thousands, it is very big. When we started attacking this wood the trees were as close as they possibly could be but you should see it now you can see straight through it quite clear. Devil's Wood is another sight I could tell you something about but what happened to me in this wood I think it will be best not to tell you as it was too horrible to mention, I shall not forget it to my last day.

It is impossible for me to try and describe to you what these woods look like after a battle, there are hundreds of things I could tell you which 9 out of 10 would say were all lies, it is only those who have seen them that would believe. I have heard a lot of men say that if Hell is a worse place than this I shall turn religious, these are places where hundreds of men have said their prayers who have never said them before.

This war is teaching people a lot of things that they never gave a thought to before. I will just tell you one little thing that happened to me on the Somme in the early hours of 14th September, just a very few words only – I was wet to the skin, no overcoat, no water sheet, I had about 3 inches of clay clinging to my clothes and it was cold, I was in an open dugout and do you know what I did – I sat down in the mud and cried, I do not think I have cried like I did that night since I was a child. . . .

It was four days after the officially recorded end of the Battle of the Somme that Sweeney came near to being taken prisoner, when a German raiding party stormed the trenches, no doubt seeking a haul of prisoners for identification and interrogation purposes.

. . . We had been wondering why Fritz had been so quiet for four days when at 3.15 a.m. on the 21st we were awakened in our dugout (myself, my Sgt Major and 2 other officers' servants) by the noise of a lot of shells bursting. The Sgt Major went up into the trench to see what was the matter, that left myself and the 2 other servants in the dugout. We could hear the shells were now falling farther back, the German guns having risen, a few minutes after this we heard a 'Bang' on our stairs which led down to our dugout – we guessed in a second what had happened – I grasped hold of my rifle and got at one corner of the stair the other 2 got to the other entrance.

We heard some strange voices shouting and they then began to throw more bombs down but we were safe enough as long as we kept clear of the stairs. Presently I heard someone coming down, I shouted 'Who are you' he said something but I pulled my trigger and he said no more, only he rolled down to me with 2 very much alive ones following him up, but they stood no chance once they were on the stairs. I let go at them, one I killed the other died later, the other 2 servants shot five, one wounded. A little later I heard some very welcome voices, our own lads and the Captain's. The Captain was very pleased as we had saved a book called the 'Log Book' which is very secret and contains a lot of valuable information . . .

Fritz took 15 Lincolns and 18 Northumberland Fusiliers back to Germany with them. The only casualties the Germans suffered were in our dugout, 3 of us had killed 8 of them. Myself and the 2 servants have been in front of the General who said all sorts of nice things to us but gave us 'nothing' only one of his cigarettes. One of the Germans I killed had a fine gold watch on him but I did not have the pluck to take it from him but our Captain did.

The German that I shot who died afterwards was a fine

84

looking man I was there when he died poor chap. I did feel sorry but it was my life or his, he was speaking but none of us could understand a word he said, to tell you the truth I had a tear myself, I thought to myself perhaps he has a Mother or Dad also a sweetheart and a lot of things like that, I was really sorry I did it but God knows I could not help myself. . . .

For Sweeney there was another year in and out of the trenches before that longed-for 'Blighty one' sent him home for good. Luck (or God as he would have put it) was with him. Not least when he was sent on leave just before his battalion went into action on the Ypres front at the start of the final assault on the Passchendaele Ridge. On 4 October 1917 380 out of 660 men in his battalion were killed or missing.

It was during this leave that Jack and Ivy became engaged. Mrs Sweeney recalls that she had by now come to know him and love him through his letters and that she had no hesitation in accepting. Her parents so warmly approved that they put a spare room at his disposal. He spent his last night there, nearly missing his train early next morning through oversleeping. Back at the front this, and other, moments of his leave-taking are still fresh in his mind:

. . . Yes Darling I expected that you would be worrying about me the day I left home as I did make a little noise going downstairs in a hurry, so Mum heard me I bet she guessed that I was late as it was daylight. I dressed in 5 minutes that morning. I should have so much liked to have said goodbye to you that morning as I did feel miserable knowing that I had lost my train to St Pancras and also thinking I had lost it at Victoria but I was alright as soon as I found that I was in time at Victoria although I felt it when

I saw the other boys with their girls on the platform, but still I wiped my eyes and fancied that you were there. . . .

Yes dearest I understand about the last evening we spent together in the drawing room, I am glad that you did not cry dear but I must tell you dear that I was crying myself that morning I came downstairs past your room and I had a good mind to come in and say goodbye but I thought at the time that it would be very wrong of me to do that so I passed on and I glanced into the drawing room at the spot where we sat the night before. Well darling I should not get sad when you are in the drawing room just think of the happy times we had there dear also put the record on, the one where the Policeman is on point duty. O yes darling I feel it just the same being parted from you dear but as you say dear we may be together sooner than we expected. . . .

What do the boys say about me getting engaged? Some say lucky kid, others Poor Old Nobbler *caught at last* – Sgt O'Brien I have not had a chance to speak to yet but I can guess what he will say, Très Bon, when's the wedding. . . .

When Sweeney rejoined his battalion, the Third Battle of Ypres was floundering to a close after three months' of the most appalling fighting in history. Sweeney heads his letters 'Somewhere in the Mud' and, though he had escaped the nightmare of going into action over that ghastly morass of a battlefield, he is moved and angered as never before.

. . . If only the people of England could have seen what I saw yesterday they would not grumble about the air raids. I had to go to – and I saw some terrible sights. I saw motor lorries sunk in the mud over the wheels, also horses with just part of their heads showing above the swamp, also 2 tanks which were in the Push and were buried – the men who were still in them will never be able to tell the tale of the fight but they were heroes. And the dead – well I have never seen so many dead before, mostly Germans, we are burying them as quickly as possible but the weather has been so bad that we have been unable to get at some of them and a lot have been buried in the bogs that will account for so many men who are missing. . . .

The Menin Road is a cobbled road or was before the shells smashed it up and each side is just like the marshes near the River Lee, the sights up there are terrible, on each side of the road there are dead horses and men, carts motor lorries etc. in the hundreds. The Somme was bad enough but this is a thousand times worse.

Well darling it is not right for me to tell you of all these horrors but perhaps you don't mind as I am only telling you what the Papers are forbidden to tell – the TRUTH. Yes the Censor if he reads this letter may say that I am chancing my arm for sending this news, all I can say to him is let the papers publish what the troops out here are really doing also the torture they are going through, then perhaps the public will realise that a man out here in the fighting forces deserves better treatment than he gets.

There are men now in the trenches full of water who are nearly dead, they are fast dying of cold they go sick see the doctor go back and try to stick it until they get relieved. Mind you dear I am not running our doctor down he is a good man but he has his orders from the others above him. When the men do get relieved some of them find that they are too ill to walk back to where the regiment is going and they have to stop for a rest and while resting on the road they may be hit by shrapnel and taken on a stretcher to the dressing station, that is if we have any brave stretcher bearers who are willing to risk their lives – it is every man for himself on this road. . . .

We had a hell of a time going up to relieve another regiment. It was a black night and we could not see the man in front of us, we were just leaving the road to start on the trench boards when 2 shells came killing 12 men and wounding 30 in my company. What was left of us got onto the boards and went as fast as we could but that was as quick as a snail for if we missed the board we would go into the mud.

Try and picture it dear yourself, on the board and Fritz dropping shells and you dare not go back you might run into a shell so you just go forward, there is no place to take cover and it is terrible. I have thanked God for sparing me. . . .

It was on the Cambrai front a month later that Sweeney had final cause for thanksgiving. By now all his old mates had been killed or wounded. He was the oldest man in his company, a company composed entirely of conscripts ('men who have been slacking in England until they were fetched') and inexperienced young officers for whom he had neither sympathy nor respect. 'I would like to put in for my Commission' he wrote in a dejected letter to Ivy 'but am afraid I am not a good enough scholar.'

His unexpected release from it all came through the agency of another German raiding party. He writes about it to Ivy in the comparative luxury of a hospital ward in Rouen, where 'the sisters are very nice and the beds are lovely.'

. . . The snow had started to fall and about 4.20 a.m. I heard a lot of shouting on the right of our post (held by 26 men). I guessed what had happened and jumped on the fire step and by my side were 7 men and a machine gun. I saw 5 Germans not 10 yards off and was just going to fire – I believe I did fire – but just as I fired there was a blinding

88

flash and the next I remember was a horrible noise in my ears and blood running down my face.

All the other men were lying at the bottom of the trench and I felt 2 or 3 men run over me, they were Germans going through the trench. When I got up everything was quiet or so I supposed as I could not hear anything only the noise in my ears. Our reinforcements came up and cleared Fritz off. All the men in my trench were wounded but none killed I am glad to say. Fritz took 5 men back as prisoners and the machine gun. Our men were badly wounded except me . . .

Sweeney's body wounds were superficial and it was only the damage to his hearing that hung in the balance between Blighty and a return to the trenches. In the event he was given the benefit of any doubt. Hearts were evidently touched by this lean-faced veteran of twenty-nine, prematurely aged, with some of his hair turned white, who would be lucky indeed to survive a fourth year in the firing line.

Two days before Christmas 1917 (the first Christmas of the war he was to spend out of the trenches), Sweeney writes jubilantly to Ivy:

You will be surprised to hear that I am in dear old Blighty. I am posting this letter from the hospital ship. I had a special ear doctor to pass before he marked me for Blighty – my service in France helped me a lot, also the matron of the hospital at the base – God bless her. . . .

Although later in life Sweeney was to become partially deaf, requiring a hearing aid, the immediate effects of that bomb-blast soon wore off in the Devon hospital to which he was sent,

89

and within a month he had been passed as fit for duty. But his luck held. His Commanding Officer took into account that he had served three years and four months at the front and had been wounded five times and found him a job as mess orderly for the duration.

In March 1918 he married Ivy. Most of the letters he wrote to her from then until his discharge from the army in March 1919 have been retained by Mrs Sweeney as being 'private and personal love letters'. Typical of the few she included in the collection for the Imperial War Museum is one written shortly after their marriage which begins 'My own darling wife', ends 'Millions of kisses, tons of love, I am always your ever loving Old Bean, Jack,' and echoes that reliance on her that had grown with every letter that had passed between them during their long correspondence:

. . . O yes dearest what suits you I am sure will always suit me, as I am not a particular Old Bean. Yes dear I know that all you do will be to make us both happy. . . .

In the 'land fit for heroes' that never materialised, their love was tested to the full. Sweeney had intended to start a confectioner's business but they lost all their savings when their bank failed. Ivy was forced to take shorthand-typing jobs and sell all her valuables. Between the wars they had a hard struggle to bring up their family of four boys and two girls.

Their eldest daughter, Mrs Doris Finch (who was instrumental in bringing the letters to light in 1976), has early memories of standing with her father in long dole queues of underfed and poorly clothed men. 'When out of work Dad used to do the cooking, making tasty dishes out of the cheapest foods, stale cakes, crusts of bread,' she recalls. 'For some years he rented a stall in Leather Lane market, Holborn, where he sold sweets and toffees he made himself from his father's old recipes. The blitz closed that down and for the rest of the Second World War he served as an ARP warden.

'During the war two of my brothers served in the army (one rising to Captain), one in the RAF. My youngest brother and sister were evacuated with my mother to Cornwall during the blitz, and it was during our time together then that I learned from my father for the first time something of what he had been through in the First War. Because of his experiences in the trenches he had a very acute ear for the sound of bombs coming down. On one occasion he pulled me into a shelter in the nick of time.'

Of the husband she has never ceased to mourn since his death, Ivy Sweeney says, 'He was always so very gentle and kind, a wonderful father, and I loved him dearly.' She now lives alone in a flat in Leytonstone, not far from Maude Terrace where she and Jack first met. In her bedroom stands the steel-lined army chest Jack acquired as a young regular, in which the scores of letters he had written to her in those terrible years of war lay undisturbed during his lifetime.

There was one among them Mrs Sweeney chose to end her own edited version to be read by their children and children's children. It tells how Jack Sweeney celebrated the end of the war, a war in which he had felt no great enmity for the Germans he was trained to kill and in which most of his 'poor dear old chums' had given their lives so that victory bells could peal and flags fly.

Old Mill,
Cuckney,
Nr Mansfield, Notts
12 November 1918

When we got the good news of the end of the WAR yesterday I was passing the church with another man when the

Flag went up over the church and the parson told us that all the bell-ringers were at work so six of us got together and we rang them or at least made a terrible noise for an hour and then we went and had a drink.

I got a big flag and nearly broke my neck – I climbed to the top of the roof where the German prisoners were and stuck it up and it will stay there now as no one will chance going up to get it down. The prisoners were as excited as we were. . . .

Chapter 4

Reflections
of a Brass Hat

'Brass hats', 'blimps', 'base wallahs' — staff officers at their comfortable headquarter billets at a safe distance from the firing line in the First World War were invariably referred to in such derogatory terms by the men enduring the hardships and hazards of the trenches. But, apart from the generals directly responsible for the prosecution of the war, they rarely feature in histories and first-hand accounts. Shadowy figures, they are akin to the back-stage staff of a theatre, indispensable to a production but out of the limelight.

Major Charles Lionel Atkins Ward-Jackson spent over three years on the Western Front, for most of the time as Camp Commandant to VII Corps, and the daily letters he wrote to his wife 'Queenie' reveal an engaging personality far removed from the popular conception of a brass hat as blinkered fuddy-duddy or pompous martinet.

A Territorial Army officer, rooted in the sporting traditions of the Victorian and Edwardian landed gentry, he writes about the war as a 'show' that could on occasion be grippingly exciting, more often boring, and in which he is only too aware that his role is an insignificant one. Whilst hobnobbing with generals on easy, sometimes familiar terms, he has none of the Regular Army officer's preoccupation with preferment, protocol, spit-and-polish. He writes perceptively, often critically,

93

about the progress of the war, but his letters are primarily a sharing of experiences with a wife whose companionship he sorely misses. Lively with gossip and anecdote, imbued with a sense of humour, they are entertaining even when his far-from-onerous duties lead him to complain 'how awful it is to waste one's time like this'.

That Ward-Jackson was a man who inspired affection as well as respect is clear from an obituary tribute paid by a friend in The Times *after his death in 1930 at the age of sixty-one. 'Our lives were brightened by his entry and left darker by his passing. . . . No one had a keener, nor pleasanter sense of humour, and I have never seen him more merry than when the laugh was against himself. He could sing an Irish or a hunting song as well as any one; he stored up amusing incidents and remarks which he collected in his associations with local characters, and was interested in the history, folk-lore, dialect and antiquities of his county. He loved his garden. In his hunting days he was a first flight man to hounds, and rode well in point-to-point races; he was a good four-in-hand whip, good with rod and gun, and at almost every game that can be mentioned. A brave and gentle, a delightful and cheerful, spirit has left us. . . .'*

It was because of what might be described as an accident of birthplace that Ward-Jackson was enabled to lead a life of leisure (apart from the Army, and later Parliament, he never held a salaried position). Rich deposits of iron ore had been discovered on the family estate, Normanby Hall, in Cleveland, Yorkshire. From his Yorkshire father (his mother was Irish), who died when he was young, he inherited a sizeable fortune, which only dwindled later in life, partly due to the generous scale of his hospitality.

After leaving Eton Ward-Jackson joined the Territorials, spent some time as aide-de-camp to the Governor of Ceylon, and served in the Boer War with the Yorkshire Hussars, being twice mentioned in dispatches. In 1908, at the age of thirty-

seven, he married Florence Olga ('Queenie') Bennett, aged twenty-five. Because of the increasing encroachments of Teeside industrialisation, he moved from fifteen-bedroomed Normanby Hall to rent a much larger mansion at Shobdon in Herefordshire.

There, with a large retinue of servants, the Ward-Jacksons entertained lavishly. It was a life-style of sporting pursuits and house parties that paid unexpected dividends for Ward-Jackson during the war. His letters to his wife are peppered with references to mutual friends and acquaintances, caught up like him in the war machine, with whom he could temporarily forget the grim present in nostalgic reminiscence of the good old days at Normanby Hall and Shobden.

William Ward-Jackson, a nephew of Ward-Jackson, has only dim boyhood recollections of his uncle – his charm, his elegance ('I have never seen a man wear good clothes with such panache'), his sporting prowess. He vividly recalls his aunt, who died in 1947.

'She was a sweet brunette, slight, rather shy and vulnerable, and we all loved her. Because of poor sight, and a disinclination to wear spectacles, she used a lorgnette, described in the letters as a monocle. She was probably more intelligent than Charlie and certainly had greater powers of concentration. She was great on paper work and, if she had not been brought up in an absurdly protected way, would have been a first class accountant.'

The marriage was childless, to her deep distress, and most of her husband's letters are addressed to her mother's riverside house on the Thames at Bourne End, Mill House, where she spent most of the war. None of her letters to him have survived, but there is evidence that they would have shown as close and intelligent an interest in his progress as she was to display during his four years as Conservative Coalitionist MP for Leominster just after the war (The Times obituarist refers to her 'devoted and eloquent help in his political and parliamentary life').

On occasions, indeed, Queenie's own interpretation of the way things are going, or should be going, draws from her husband a mild rebuke:

. . . How amusing for you to tell me all about the Battle of Ypres. We are not taking any active part in it, but we are in the show anyway! So we could possibly give you a hint or two instead of the other way. . . .

. . . You talk of stale-mate as if this show could get a 'move on' during the next ten years. Nobody out here thinks anything at all about the Russians. We don't consider them worth a damn. . . .

. . . Your letter has just arrived. It isn't at all a good thing that the Boche have taken the offensive. . . .

But most personal references tell of a woman much missed:

. . . How you would love being in this show! There is not a single thing which would not interest you enormously and that poor old monocle of yours would soon be quite worn out! . . .

. . . Two letters from you this morning and they made me so happy and you write so sweetly that they are my greatest joy and I look forward to the mail with such impatience when it is late. . . .

. . . My mare Dinah has been seedy again but is now pulling round. I love her for herself because she is such a dear, but I love her still more because I hope she will be yours one of these fine days. . . .

. . . It is Sunday and the church bells are ringing. How I wish you and I were just going across the Court Yard into our little Shobden Church. . . .

The letters came to light, on offer in a dealer's catalogue, in the form of a bound typescript volume of 731 pages, evidently produced by Queenie Ward-Jackson after her husband's death (obituary notices are included) and with the beginning and end of each letter omitted. They were snapped up by the Imperial War Museum as giving a rare view of the war from the vantage point of a highly literate headquarters officer, with no axe to grind, a ready pen and no inhibitions about rank or title.

The tone is set in Ward-Jackson's first letter, after arriving near the Ypres front by train from Le Havre. He tells his wife he has shared a compartment with his two great friends Charlie (Earl of Feversham) and Harry (Viscount Lascelles) and has just been introduced to the Commander of the Division, 'a very decent comfortable old body seemingly'.

In these egalitarian days Ward-Jackson would undoubtedly be decried as a snob. He can write about Guards officers that 'they all look like gentlemen' and about the Tommy (when not in action) that he is 'a rascal and a lazy lout'. But he is no sycophant. His most vehement denunciations are aimed at the top brass on the Imperial General Staff and in the War Cabinet, whom he variously describes as 'old wastrels', 'old washerwomen' and 'blithering old dough-headed antiques'.

From a typescript amounting to over 350,000 words, dating from April 1915 to February 1918, the section from which the following extracts have been taken is that relating to the Battle of the Somme. Comparing Ward-Jackson's account with that of Private Sweeney in the preceding chapter, it is difficult to believe they are engaged in the same event. To Ward-Jackson in his headquarters château, the nightmare of that assault

97

across no-man's-land and the ensuing ebb and flow of battle are reduced to voices on a telephone and a changing of flags on a map.

Ward-Jackson's disjointed references to the actual battle come as an anticlimax to his descriptions of the build up to it. In these he seems to touch the pulse of history, to transmit the awesome thrill of anticipation as men and materials mass for the kill. Fifteen months before, on the eve of the Second Battle of Ypres, he had expressed the same wonder at 'the huge enormous scale of it all'. Only later, when confusion and carnage had set in, did he reflect on 'what it all means – an enormous amount of casualties on both sides for an odd kilometre of ground, utter misery caused to civilians, and as soon as one battle comes to an end, another begins on exactly the same lines.'

In June 1916 all that seems forgotten. The month before he had been joined by Queenie on a short leave in Paris. Now in comfortable quarters in the unscathed town of Pas, the Corps headquarters, with two batmen to attend to his needs (and those of his mare Dinah), a staff car to transport him on duty and social calls, a recently arrived Fortnum and Mason hamper from home to add delicacies to his table, and above all this excitement in the air heralding the Great Event, life was good.

20 June. More than anything else I would like you to be here for a few hours. Everything is quite quiet and you would think nothing was happening or going to happen to make the whole place hideous, unless I could take you out towards the front to see all the wonderful sights. Everywhere there are troops; under every bank there are horses; Field Ambulance Hospitals are everywhere; huge howitzers on railway-trucks lurk stealthily in orchards; telegraph and telephone wires on flimsy stakes like hop-poles cross each other in every direction and make a sort of Aerial entangle-

ment overhead.

The ground trembles with great convoys of motor-lorries bringing up ammunition to the dumps; and over all, serenely disregarding our Archies, sails majestically a flight of German aeroplanes, a much more elegant machine to look at than ours or the French, and appearing almost transparent, like Lohengrin's swans, in the blue sky. They are at a height where we cannot reach them with our guns, over twelve thousand feet.

With such instruments as the allies possess, no reconnaissance would be any good, for objects on the earth are too small at a height like that to pick up. But with the Boche it is different. He relies on his lens in his camera which is altogether in a class by itself and which shows, so they say, even at twelve thousand feet every vehicle on the road. All is constrained bustle and action. Countless streams of GS wagons pass the end of this street on their way, laden with great logs of poplar, to the dug-outs for the guns, and as for ammunition convoys, they never cease day or night.

My motor-bus daily brings from the forward villages parties of officers and men for an hour or two practice at a village in the back area, in storming the enemy's lines and wire, for an exact copy of the sector of Boche trench which each platoon will at some date have to attack is prepared for them in the back area to practise on. A splendid idea.

I want to find some tree up which I can climb and make a little platform so that I can see with my glasses something of what is happening. I don't only mean the blasting into the air of huge clouds of earth, but the actual movements of the troops, if that be possible, and I don't get plumb in the way of the Boche 'Crumpers'. But I think their guns will be sufficiently occupied on shelling our front trenches. They will not have much time to pick out places in the back line or try and register on batteries. It will all be wonderfully thrilling and the noise will be tremendous. Major Bowles, our Staff Officer to GOC, RA, thinks the Boches will move off and we shall waste all our shells. A nice prospect!

21 June. After tea yesterday evening Anderson, Wickham and I drove into Doullens to see the IInd Corps which had just arrived there. . . . One of the officers I talked to had been in a Division next door to one of the new Anzac Corps. He said they are fine fellows but absolutely undisciplined. They go making small ventures amongst themselves, a platoon or so, to raid a German trench without telling their staff or anyone, and not even warning their Gunners not to fire on a particular spot. The other night they had a fine mix up. They got amongst the Boches, and Boche gas and all were muddled up together with Boche guns and all were playing on the lot at the same time. It was unpleasant enough while it lasted to cause them to desist from these vagaries for a time. . . .

22 June. . . . I cannot remember whether I told you about Hunter Weston and the speech? The 11th Brigade in the 4th Division had two regular regiments taken away from it, and two more were to be selected to replace them. Two of the Warwickshire Territorials from the 48th Division were chosen and as they marched down the road towards the 4th Division Hunter Weston stopped them close to Marieux. With them was the Irish Padre, Macready, about whom I have often written to you, telling you how he would sometimes make all the men shake with laughter in his sermons, and how excitable and emotional he was. He halted with the men, whilst the officers went forward, and listened to General Hunter Weston's remarks to them.

Immediately afterwards the men were formed up for a speech from the General. He said: 'Men of Warwickshire, men of the gallant 48th Territorial Division of which you are justly proud, you have been selected to join the 11th Brigade of the Regular Army. This is the Brigade, the mention even of whose name brings a thrill to England! This is a Brigade which has performed prodigies of valour and endurance since it came out with the original Expeditionary Force. This Brigade was mine and you can hold your heads up with greater pride than ever since you now belong to the 11th Brigade.

'Soon you will be called upon for the supreme effort of the soldier. Very soon the word will come to you that you will be expected to break through the lines of the Foe. Be not afraid; there is plenty behind you, plenty to give you support. I say, Be not afraid; leap over the parapet! Kill the Germans! Kill them ALL! Spike them! Stab them! Stick your bayonets into them!'

This was too much for our Padre Macready. He happened to be standing, with his eyes starting from their sockets with excitement, right in front of the General and in a frenzy he leapt into the air twirling his shillelagh round his head and burst out into the wildest Irish HURROO! He electrified the men who cheered wildly too, and Hunter Weston, saluting and bowing his thanks, was led off by ADC's orderlies, flags and everything else besides!

Of course he is rather theatrical and that sort of thing but as Stevenson says in *The British Admirals*, 'You do want some of the panoply and circumstance of war when you want to enthuse.' The fact that the General made an equally impassioned address to the Divisional Band on the occasion of their last performance outside his Château at dinner-time does seem to come rather like an anti-climax however. . . .

23 June. Yesterday afternoon I went with Wickham to see the arrangements made for traffic control and the reception of prisoners of war forward. We sat with one of the traffic

control officers in a village about a mile from the trenches, and a sixty pounder Battery was popping off every minute or two quite close to the back yard, and shaking all the glass in the windows and making the whole place rattle. After about an hour the old gun got on my nerves and I went round to the Battery and told the officer to stop as he was disturbing me. He only laughed. I had given him leave for England a fortnight ago, and I told him if he loosed off again he would get no more leave from me! But if that one sixty pounder Battery makes all that row in the village, what will it be like on *Der Tag*! . . .

26 June. Yesterday was a day of great excitement. We had a service as usual at 10.15 at the Château yard where were the Corps Commander and General Lyon and several others. We heard a good deal of gun fire and guessed that aeroplanes were about but nobody took much notice. However – crash! bang! And we heard the splinters and things flying past the door of the coach-house where we all were. General Lyon spoke a word to the Corps Commander, who nodded, and then to the Padre, and we stopped the service just when we got to the second hymn and were singing:

> 'Lead us, Heavenly Father, lead us
> O'er the world's tempestuous sea,
> Guard us, Guide us, Keep us, Feed us
> For we have no help but Thee.'

Notwithstanding this last line the Corps Commander said 'You'd all better scatter.' And so we did. There were about nineteen German Aeroplanes but of course none of ours dare tackle them. Altogether they dropped about half-a-dozen bombs here killing two of our RE, wounding seven, wounding one girl and her father, and killing one horse, one hen and one pigeon.

It was a very nasty sensation while it lasted and there is no doubt that we were very lucky at the Château and the hymn was really justified. For the bomb was carrying on straight for the Château when it hit and exploded in the top of a big beech tree, of which it cut off several branches, but it did no further damage. The Boches had already bombed two railway stations and our casualty clearing station.

However in the afternoon Wickham and I went down towards the Front and got on an eminence some three or four thousand yards from the trenches right opposite Gommecourt Wood which is the main objective of our bombardment. It certainly was a most cheering sight to the soldiers and indeed to myself. Guns of every size and calibre were exploding their shells in this wood and all around it. A 15 inch on our left paid special attention to its right hand corner and one on our right to its left hand corner, and as these detonated a huge patch of ground about as big as Betty's rose garden seemed to rise bodily in the air in a great column of smoke higher than the poplar trees by your temple. You cannot imagine what an inferno it must have been in that place.

All night too it went on whilst the field guns devoted themselves to hammering all the roads in the rear in order to make the question of reinforcements and supplies difficult. And it was not over our part of the show only but far away to the right was a crumbling and a booming like distant thunder save that it never for an instant ceased. And all night long the sky was illuminated with bright flashes far away as the eye could reach, and every now and then sounded the deep bass cough of the huge howitzers in our area as they threw their half-ton of destruction against the German position, each one half-a-ton of revenge for their own messages at Verdun. The whole scene paralyses the imagination. . . .

GHQ are absolutely confident about this show, the Southern part of which is being done by the French. It is colossal and oh, if it only goes well it ought to finish the war, or at any rate put the beginning of the end well on its legs.

27 June. Yesterday afternoon young Butler and I rode up to a hill a good way off the trenches but commanding a panoramic view of the bombardment. It certainly was a wonderful sight. All round the semi-circle in front of us was a continuous haze of smoke from bursting shells, and the Boches were replying very heavily and adding to the din. The bombardment seems to be going on favourably but when we made a feint yesterday that we were going to attack at a particular point of the line, before one minute had elapsed the Boche had a barrage of fire put on our front line trenches. They are wonderful indeed. One never finds a flaw in their staff work or their Army management and Intelligence Department. But we are hoping that before we have done with this bombardment there will not be quite as much kick left in them as there is now for they are sticking it out in a way which nobody but they or we would do.

Last night I dined with a Company of the London Scottish who are going up to the forward area today. They are the Jumpers-off when the day arrives and they talked to me a lot about it last night. It was odd to see the different demeanours of the officers. Some consoled themselves that the Huns would do nothing to stop them at first and that another Battalion would push past them when they once got into the Boche trenches. Others thought they would be stopped by the barrage. Others said that they meant getting on and putting an end to the show. Of the three I did not know which would do best when it came to the pinch. Probably all as good as one another. . . .

I was so pleased with your letter, and I was sure you would like Hunter Weston's speech. Alfred may be right about him, but if there is one thing in the world to prevent a General winning battles, it is to be afraid of casualties. That is the awful part of war. Troops must hold on, or must attack, more indeed this war than all others, more's the pity. To raise enthusiasm a man must be human. . . .

28 June. I am busy today about the Prisoners of War Camp, up to my knees in mud, and I hear from Wright who was in the front line trenches this morning that they are simply rivers. It is pouring again now, and it is simply damnable. . . .

Our bombardment has been going on for days now and night patrols describe the appearance of the Hun's trenches as unrecognisable. And still we are keeping at it. I sincerely trust we may go on and get our tails up and the Boches' tails down. They will not take much bad news with equanimity. It must be terrible for them to sustain this bombardment, this roaring and rending and deafening din of the guns.

30 June. I still have very little news to tell you. The papers keep you informed of all that goes on that we are allowed to write about, and indeed, besides the bombardment, there have only been raids and such-like independent shows. Of course the Boche know all about it, hang them! How I wish we could scupper the lot.

I never thought the Boches would publish a report of their bombing raid on this place or I would have told you all about it when I wrote on Sunday. It did not seem to me important enough to add it to my letter of that day, so I wrote you all about it next, and by now you will have got the account, and know that it happened when we were at Morning Service. . . .

I have seen nobody outside lately, but there was rather an

excitement yesterday when two or three strange Generals appeared at Corps Headquarters. When asked what they were doing they said they were spare Generals sent down in case of casualties! Jolly for all the Brigadiers at present alive and kicking and who have no intention of getting killed or wounded! Not that they will be able to help it anyhow if it has got to happen.

It was at 7.30 the following morning, zero hour, that the British barrage suddenly lifted and all along the eighteen-mile front the first waves of infantrymen went over the top across no-man's-land. By the end of the day 993 officers and 18,247 other ranks had been killed or died of wounds. Total casualties were 57,470, almost exactly half of the 143 battalions from six Army Corps who had gone into the attack with such high hopes of a 'walk-over'.

In Ward-Jackson's account, from the headquarters of VII Corps, of the first two days of the battle there is scarcely a hint of the slaughter in progress. From hindsight it seems almost incredible that at this nerve centre of a vital sector of the front there was apparently so little grasp of the fact that all the confident predictions of the master-planners had foundered and that a massacre had ensued. One hesitates to imagine what would have been the reactions of Tommies like Private Sweeney, lucky enough to have survived, to Ward-Jackson's reference to two visitors to the Château, General Sir Douglas Haig, the Commander-in-Chief, and General Sir William Robertson, Chief of the Imperial General Staff, commiserating with the Corps Commander on his 'disappointment' at not attaining his objective.

1 July. Today is a most important day and I have to be up at the Château on duty, transmitting messages from the

front, altering maps and so on with Colonel Mildmay. So probably I shall have very few moments in which to write to you. I am not sure whether we are allowed to recount events as they happen for a special Censor-officer has been told off to examine letters. But it does not make any difference. In any case you will read accounts of things that are happening in the Press before this can possibly reach you. The last two days have been lovely and the ground has dried up nicely while there is a gentle SW breeze – just right.

We live in very exciting times and are all full of high aspirations and of enthusiasm. What German prisoners have been caught have been very miserable. One was taken opposite us the night before last and he gave a most melancholy and picturesque account of what was going on behind the Hun line. How the bombardment gave them no peace and had smashed everything to pieces, how the trenches are unrecognisable as such and not a parapet left standing, and how that he was being employed when captured on a fatigue party in the front line digging out others who had been buried in dugouts smashed by our shells. He was jolly glad to be safe and sound in our lines.

As for the prisoners the VIII Corps took yesterday, they said that the whole lot of their comrades were longing for the moment to come when we would attack so that they could surrender en masse! I only hope what they say is true. The enemy's strength is just about double in front of us what it usually is. That is what the prisoners say. So if all goes well and if luck is on our side we ought to do big things. It is now 7.35 a.m. and I shall go to the Château, and will very likely have something else to add before I finish.

(Later) We have not got on as well as we hoped. We hear good accounts in the other parts of the attack further South, but we have not progressed much, I am sorry to say.

Still there is yet time for improvement and I believe our casualties have not been very heavy. We have now about two hundred Boche prisoners in my camp near here and I have sent rations and things up to them. It was most thrilling being at the Château. I received all the messages from the different forces and took them round to the different officers so that I knew everything that happened.

2 July. I shall again be very busy at the Château today, besides which I have to attend at a Court Martial this morning. So perhaps I may not have much of a chance of writing you a long letter.

You will see by the papers that we got on very well in the South but were held up here. It would appear that the Huns suspected the weight of the attack to be somewhere not far from us and had an extra strong force to meet our attack. Anyhow we gained a lot of ground at first but lost it again afterwards though the casualties were not particularly heavy.

It was a very fine and warm day and everything was favourable. The Boches withdrew, we think, most of their forces from the front leaving only enough for a fairly firm resistance. They then waited until our fellows got on and when they had them some distance on they counter-attacked fiercely and drove them back. But the Hun is a soldier and no mistake. Their discipline is so evident everywhere. When they are being brought in as prisoners they march like as if they were in their battalions. When I sent parties down to wash yesterday from the Prisoners of War Camp – the washing place is some distance off – they immediately fell in in order, two abreast, and it was our guard that was dodging about them not knowing the proper order to fall in!

I stayed up the whole day yesterday at the Château till 12.0 last night. There won't be quite so much news today, I

108

expect, for the people in the South have reached their objective for the time being and have done very well. Great excitement in the town here amongst the people to see the '*Sales Boches*'. They all turned out in the streets, men, women and children, fearfully pleased at the sight.

(7.0 p.m.) There has been nothing doing. 'Wally' Robertson has been to the Château and the C-in-C and they have been very nice to the Corps Commander who took the disappointment of not attaining his objective very pluckily and did not fuss.

Next day Ward-Jackson rode up to his favourite eminence over-looking the battlefield. Apart from desultory shellfire, there was now nothing going on near enough for him to see. He takes the opportunity of describing what he now knows to have happened on the first day of the battle, and to muse on the impasse that has been reached in trench warfare:

. . . The terrible difficulty in modern war is to get on. Men can get into the front line trench and even penetrate some hundreds of yards and occupy others, but if there is a big resistance they must come back. The explanation of this is that the days of the rifle are over. Except in the case of three or four snipers per company with telescopic sights fitted, gone are the days when it was of any use to shoot well on the range. Artillery and machine guns and bombs, especially bombs, and rarely the bayonet, are the factors that most matter, and, almost above all, the spade. If the dug-outs are deep and strongly made enough they will withstand almost any bombardment, and incoming parties attacking are met with bombs. . . .

But it was on a personal basis that the realities of the battle came home to him:

I was dreadfully sorry to hear that Lindsey and nearly all the other fellows of the London Scottish with whom I dined the night before they went up are killed. I think out of the seven officers there is only one unwounded. I feel it very much for I think I wrote and told you what sort of an impression the Regiment as a whole gave me. There was something not exactly apprehensive but resigned about them and that sentiment was justified for they had a bad time. They were the first Battalion of our line to reach their objective over two lines of German trenches and were the last to leave it, and this they only did when bombed from the left and bombarded from the right.

They certainly were the finest and highest class of men I have ever seen in the war. One of the Sergeants created a sort of furore as he marched through the streets here. He was what the Liaison officer described as a 'Beauty', an Adonis. I saw him in the camp and had to speak to him and he looked like a big Greek god with golden hair and a rosy-freckled complexion, and a smile like an Osborne Cadet for mischief. Now he may be dead or wounded for all I know.

It was dreadfully sad about Lindsey. His widow has a little boy of four years old or thereabouts and a baby girl born last month. I said to Thorpe, the GSOI of the 46th who is the widow's cousin, that I had noticed something weird and uncanny about the London Scottish as they went up and that I could not make out quite what it was. I said this before they went into the line, when they were just going into the forward trenches, and Thorpe replied, 'If you were a Highlander you would not make that remark, they *know*.'

I was very impressed and I do not know that anything has made me feel in that sort of way so depressed as the death of my friend and all these splendid young fellows, the finest type of English. I can see them now with their pipers playing a wild skirl as they marched through this French town. The pipers with their bonnets and black-cock feathers set at a jaunty angle on their heads, squaring their shoulders and swinging their kilts so that even the little French gamins fell in on either side to keep step. And behind them a whole company of young men clean and workmanlike with their heads a little down but their expressions brave; with a smile for all the girls and their friends amongst the crowd but just a little unmistakable droop at the corners of their mouths. They made me feel sad then. . . .

It is not for another three months, when he learns that his great friend Charlie (Earl of Faversham) has been killed, that Ward-Jackson again betrays any great emotion about the mounting casualties. Attack and counter-attack are dealt with in his letters in sporting jargon ('preparing for another biff', 'bashing the old Huns', 'a very disagreeable punch'), and the Germans are seen as worthy if misguided opponents ('gallant fellows', 'real soldiers', even 'gentlemen'). With his far-from-onerous duties as Corps Commandant leaving tracts of time to fill with country jaunts, visits to fellow brass hats, chinwags with cronies, Ward-Jackson becomes increasingly bored and homesick. But there is scarcely a letter that does not have its nugget of interest. These are representative extracts:

12 July. . . . That the Huns never expected their front line system of defence to be captured is quite evident. Dick described to me his visit to Tricourt and to the German trenches there the day before yesterday. He went down to see the celebrated hospital. This is a hospital for wounded excavated by the Boches some twenty to thirty feet under-

111

ground. It is all panelled with white enamelled wood and divided into various wards, sleeping rooms for doctors and attendants, operating theatre, all modern requirements in fact, including electric light and a bathroom with hot and cold water laid on!

All this is wonderful enough in itself, but when one comes to consider that this is the front line trench, the front line trench if you please within shouting distance of our lines, one marvels at the confidence they must have had in being able to hold out for ever against any attack we might bring. . . .

13 July. It was an extraordinary sight yesterday to see the Virgin of Albert. I wonder if you have seen a photograph of it? The figure has been knocked down by a German shell and now droops at right angles from its original position from the top of the steeple. It is painted gold and the sun came out for a minute yesterday afternoon and made the poor figure a fitting object in the foreground for such a terrible background of bursting shells and huge volcanoes of dust and smoke. . . .

17 July. . . . I hear that 'Mad Morton' in our Squadron RFC, a terribly heroic boy, flew down beside a Boche Infantry Company whom he saw marching along the road and emptied two rolls of his machine gun into them at two hundred feet distance. He then rose and flew home, having done in about half of them and with his machine riddled with bullets!

Also an amusing story about one of the 56th. After the attack he lay out in no-man's-land for two days and nights living on rations taken from the dead. When asked why he had not come in the first night he said he was frightened the Germans would see him and shoot him. The second night he said he was afraid of the English shooting him thinking he was a Boche. When asked why he came in the third night he said: 'It started to rain, Sir!'

21 July. I always think as I go along in a motor round this country what joy it will be if only they will let us bring out our cars after the war and I could take you and show you all these places. You see pictures of them but they do not really convey to your mind what they are like. You want the belt of desolation of no-man's-land and the Trenches stretching on either side of them and the feeling that there are two rows of people there waiting to kill each other whose business is that and nothing else at all, nor has been for the last two years. . . .

22 July. I have nothing on earth to do for the time being. In order to keep myself occupied I am going to hold a riding-school in the evenings for officers. And they want it. When we first started off this show one never observed anyone who rode well and looked as if he did, but if one saw a bad rider one's eyes became glued at him at once as a freak. Now it is the contrary. If anyone passes this window who knows how to sit on a horse at all, I get up from my table and run and have a look. . . .

24 July. . . . General Lyon and General Ross Johnson were discussing last night the merits of the British soldier. In General Lyon's opinion the British Tommy is the worst soldier and the worst fighting man in the world. General Johnson thought that the Belgians and the Icecreamers were worse and he told a story of an Italian advance which made me simply die with laughter.

One of the great Italian attacks was to be made; the hour was fixed; the men with bombs and bayonets were waiting the scheduled moment in the trenches. As the watch-hand reached the appointed hour the officers of the Battalion leapt to their feet in the trenches, waved their swords or arms above their heads and called '*Avanti! Avanti!*' This produced no result on the men at all. The officers again waved their arms above their heads and called '*Avanti! Avanti!*' But nothing happened.

The Battalion Commander was sent for and he walked down the trench encouraging his men with those words of fervid enthusiasm so well understood by the Latin races. Having done this, he in his turn waved his arms over his head and cried '*Avanti! Avanti!*' And still nothing happened.

At last the bravest officer in the Regiment (the Austrians were a long way off) clambered out of the trench and over the parapet where he halted, faced about, and waving his arms over his head cried '*Avanti! Avanti!*' This time it had a result for no less than fifty-five of the bravest men of the Regiment put their heads up and looked over.

When they saw the Captain it was too much for their pent-up emotions. They commenced to applaud and clap their hands vigorously, shouting '*Brava Capitano! Brava Capitano!*' And with that, stepped down amongst their more cautious comrades to bid them be inspired with such an exhibition of magnificent bravery. And nothing more happened! I have done nothing else but laugh at this story for twenty-four hours. It really is killing. . . .

26 July. . . . I cannot make out what is going to happen about Ireland. It seems to me the only solution is to patch up some temporary arrangement for the period of the war, and afterwards take a census and a vote of the whole population. If they decide on Home Rule, let them have it and no exclusion, and let them fight it out if they want to amongst themselves. Let the Ulster Division get back first though before they start scrapping. Give them no money or

anything and stop all arms going into the Country. Fists and Shillelaghs will be the best weapons for them always. The Irishman does not like a gun or a rifle at all. . . .

31 July. . . . Anderson and I were tremendously impressed with the Guards. We see one way or another at this half-way house all sorts of troops of every kind, Cavalry, Infantry, Gunners, Regulars, Territorials and New Army. But we had not seen the Guards. You never saw such a difference. In the first place the officers all looked like gentlemen, and the men twice the size, and in the second their discipline is extraordinary. Different altogether from all other regulars. Not a man sits down as you pass, no matter how far off you may be.

Harry [Viscount Lascelles] told me they have a splendid dodge. If on the march they pass any men lying about who belong to other units and who do not salute the Commanding officer, they call them up and compel them to come along with them till the next halt which may be a couple of miles or so on. They are then brought before the CO, told off, and sent about their business. He said that in the Salient everyone saluted after the Guards had been there for a bit, Canadians and everyone else. No one wanted to go two miles or so out and two miles back just for the fun of being told off at the finish. . . .

1 August. It was such fun having Harry over here to dinner last night. We talked of pleasant things like you and unpleasant things like bounders and about the War and peace and fortunes and poverty and everything in the world besides. I like him very much indeed. . . .

5 August. . . . All sorts of people from Brigadier Generals to Subalterns and Troopers blow into this office during the day asking about something or other. Some of them come

115

just when I have gone out riding and stay solidly here till I return, it may be two or three hours later. But I am heartily sick of the whole thing, to tell you the truth. I sort of feel that I am getting on in years and wasting my time in this blasted show. The months and years pass by so quickly and the summer seems to have left us almost before it started and politically we seem to be no nearer the end of the war than we were two years ago today. It is horrid.

6 August. . . . We caught a very brave Boche prisoner yesterday by a piece of very bad luck for him and we are all very sick about it. He came over yesterday morning from his own lines with a list of the wounded and unwounded prisoners whom we lost on the 1st July on this Corps front. He got as far as our wire and fixed the list up there and then turned to go back. But not seeing or hearing anyone about in our trenches he returned to our wire and crawled through it with the paper.

Unfortunately he met a covering party of ours and was stopped. He tried to explain to them what his mission was but could not make them understand. He held his hands above his head and then vigorously shook his head to show he did not mean to surrender, but all to no purpose. He was brought along to Brigade Headquarters. Of course he had then seen too much and we could not let him go back again. So we are sending over a message to be dropped by aeroplane telling his Company Commander how it happened and that we are sorry we cannot send the man over. Of course we have not questioned him about things his side, it would not be playing the game at all. . . .

10 August. The King came and stopped a minute or two with us yesterday. The Prince of Wales was with him and Derek Keppel and the usual crowd. The King looked very well. Much better than I have seen him look since the

beginning of the war, and quite cheery too. He had been all over the area and went away with General Allenby in his car. The Prince of Wales is tremendously popular. They all say he is simply a top-hole boy and the men all love him. He goes down and bathes in the mill-pool not far off our old billets every day with all the men and officers too. He has a car of his own of course which is looked upon as a perk by the 2nd Grenadier Guards officers. He has a sort of special appointment with Cavan's Corps and looks after the ammunition returns etc., and they all love him. . . .

12 August. This is the 12th August and here I am sitting in an office at 7.15 in the morning writing you a letter instead of talking to you and thinking of the glorious day's sport we are going to have on the moors. Isn't it sickening? . . .

14 August. The children's fête went off yesterday simply splendidly. Everyone enjoyed themselves hugely and it was quite the loveliest day of the year so far. The Corps Commander was very pleased with the show and went bundling about amongst the kids. . . . In the evening the young women of the town had a go at the swings and things after the children had done. Lord Cole, who talks French very well, kept chaffing everybody and the whole scene was one of real good laughing.

One thing distresses me very much and that is the way so many women are neglecting or being cruel to their husbands who are fighting out here. I censor a lot of letters every day and never a one passes without perhaps a dozen agonized appeals from the poor fellows to their wives imploring them to write and tell them that they do care for them still even if they, the wives, haven't written for two months.

And they keep asking about their children. Very often they have to appeal to a friend to tell them if their own children are all right. It is cruel in the extreme. If I had my way I would let them all go home on leave and arm them with the finest and stiffest and most tingling birch-rods possible to procure, and let them show their old women that there is some vigour in the old arms yet, even if their owners have had to be here for a year or more. They are perfect devils. . . .

15 August. . . . General Woollcombe came and dined last night with me and we had a top-hole dinner. The driver of Colonel Mildmay's car brought some fish back from Boulogne and the most delicious melon that ever was grown arrived from that darling Betty. Wasn't it lucky? Both he and his son are delightful. . . .

17 August. The weather is quite lovely with a gentle breeze from the SW. How glorious it must be in Scotland. It makes my mouth positively water to think of it, and I curse and damn these Boches to all the Blazes of Hades. I love my *David Copperfield*. Even after reading a few quite good books by modern writers lately one opens one's Dickens and finds a different business altogether. There is the touch of the master hand even if it is all so exaggerated and even if little Davey is the most advanced and precocious of children gifted with intuition and tact far beyond his years. . . .

18 August. . . . The King's visit was kept so profound a secret here that hardly any of the Staff knew of it and his movements were notified entirely by code. The Third Army hardly dared look about they were so afraid of showing something exciting in their expressions. Imagine their dismay when at eleven o'clock the morning before the King visited them, the town crier of St Pol with his drum went round the town crying '*Oyez; oyez; Citoyens de St Pol.*

19 August. I had such an enjoyable dinner at the Army Commander's house yesterday evening. General Sillem had invited my dear old friend Anderson to meet me and we had a great talk; and a most ferocious argument too over dessert in which General Holland, RA, General Kenyon, RE, and I on one side of the table ranged ourselves against General Bols, General Staff, and Lord Dalmeny, with General Sillen chipping in every now and again against our side. The argument concerned the British Tommy.

Dalmeny said there was not a soldier who would not clear out now from the war to do any sort of work, not necessarily to help the Country. General Sillem said that thousands of people on the brink of starvation had joined the Army. Offer them a decent wage and every one would clear out even if it allowed the Germans in, but they would not think of that.

General Bols said he did not see, and for the life of him could not make out, why any private soldier in the world fought at all. He supposed it was because the man was ignorant about it all before he enlisted. General Holland said he had known plenty of patriotic soldiers who fought for patriotism and who wanted to stay in the army to fight for their country. He, however, unfortunately could not name any when General Bols asked if they had come under his personal experience.

I said that everyone had some ideals. It did not matter how poor they were or how near to starvation, they had their ideals somewhere in them. And in the case of fighting it seemed that there was a collective idealism rather than an individual one. One would see a whole meeting turn from supineness to energy and any amount of men joining up who had not done so before. That one of the most remarkable things about the voluntaryism of the earlier days of the

119

war was the effect which bad news had upon recruiting. It invariably acted as a stimulus.

And as far as Tommy ever wanting to fight if he knew anything about the risk or the discomfort, I asked General Bols how he accounted for the fact that a neighbour would go and attack a burglar who was playing the devil in the next house to him, even if he had no interest whatever in the house personally. What he wanted to do was to keep the foe out and wallop him and hand him over to the police.

Dalmeny said there were many men in England who maintained that they were indifferent to whether they were governed by King George or Kaiser William or President Wilson. I said go and ask them now. I got quite cross with Dalmeny. He is very cynical and sneers at all sorts of senti-ment, but probably he only thinks so sometimes. . . .

20 August. . . . Fuller says that as he has progressed from a Brigade through Division and Corps up to Army he finds intelligence progresses in inverse ratio. The higher you get up the more stupidity and incompetence and ineptitude you find.

In a discussion with the General Staff of the Army one officer actually put forward the suggestion that the men attacking a trench should proceed across no-man's-land on hands and knees! That is not an easy means of progression for any but young brats, but to think of grown-up soldiers with rifle, two hundred rounds of ammunition and all their kit crawling about like monkeys is on the stiff side. Added to which the word of command of an officer in such tense moments as these is difficult to bring to every man in the noise and the din and the danger, so there would not be much chance of him effecting his command to a great extent with his head on the ground like a young porker. . . .

27 August. Here is another Sunday come round, the last in August 1916, the last in the whole summer, and I have never seen my own home since the bleak winds of March; not a flower or a tree except in this accursed country which one longs with every fibre of one's being and every beat of one's heart never to see again. How awful it is to waste one's time like this. One knows easy and contented moments, but never a happy one except when one dreams that one is not here at all. . . .

30 August. . . . It is simply pouring again now. I am trying to get a car to take me over to Dick Woodroffe and get information from him where Charlie Feversham is. It is not the sort of day for people to go on excursions to the trenches or for the Staff to go sailing about the front line, for with this wind and mist we can see nothing. So perhaps I shall manage it and can see the dear old chap. I had a letter from him begging me to run over if possible and see him. He tells me that he went home on special leave for 'Urgent Private Affairs'. Incidentally he put in a few days grouse-shooting which, to his huge disgust, was duly notified to all and sundry in the *Yorkshire Post*: 'The Earl of Feversham and a distinguished party were out on Tuesday shooting over the famous Helmsley Moors, etc!' He was throughly upset about it and would have liked to discover the editor in the garb of a nice fat German just heading for the bayonets of the Yeoman Rifles.

31 August. . . . Charlie and I had a great buck and he asked after you and asked a thousand and one things about the staff and everything. Like all regimental officers he thinks it makes no difference whether there is any staff or not, though he is not quite so bigoted as some of them. He is such a dear and I loved seeing him even if I had the most awful drive to get to him. . . .

121

4 September. . . . I have had rather a lot of bother lately with the old permanent-base men. Most of them are old soldiers and know how to be a great nuisance besides being decrepit. What on earth the Government keeps such old blighters out here for at all beats me. However I suppose it is always the way and you find everywhere men who have not got the energy, who are too self-indulgent, to do anything at all. It is to me quite extraordinary and there is no doubt that the British Tommy is more inclined that way than any other man in the world. He is a rascal and a lazy lout and takes no trouble to learn or to do things. How comes it that he gets on top?

I cannot but think it is really something of the ruling class about him. It is like the white overseer with the niggers; he is by nature fitted to see that the work is done and they are by nature fitted to do it. Do you think that is the case with the Germans and that a good kick from the British will always send them to their kennels with a snarl and their tail between their legs? It honestly looks like this I think. I can see no other reason for us winning as I expect we shall do, except the superiority of the British.

11 September. We keep on shoving along as you see from day to day, and the alterations of the bit of worsted and the drawing pins on my map are a tremendous event in the town. The villagers and soldiers crowd round like anything to see what has happened. Of course it looks slow work but I dare say things may hurry up a bit one of these fine days with any luck at all. . . .

14 September. In the opinion of our Chiefs out here the great decisive moment is on hand. . . . You will have lots to interest you in the papers from now on, and I expect to see even more than the usual crowds around my map at the

top of the street. Everything seems full of hope and everyone prophesying the downfall of the Huns. . . .

The 'decisive moment' was the third full-scale attempt since the launching of the Somme offensive to break through the German defences. Like the others it resulted in heavy casualties for minimal territorial gains. But 15 September 1916 remains a landmark in the history of warfare. The day the tank first went into action.

A closely-guarded British secret, thirty-six Mark I tanks spearheaded the attack. Only eleven of them succeeded in crossing the German front line, the remainder breaking down, being ditched or shot up. But, as Ward-Jackson relates, there was no doubt about the shock effect on the enemy of these 'great megalosaurus-looking beasts' lumbering ahead of the British infantry.

16 September. Yesterday was a great day entirely. In the morning I went over to see Dick Woodroffe and learn how things were going on. He had just come from seeing the C-in-C and opened his telegrams in my presence. What we were all so crazy to hear about were the 'tanks'. We knew they were to take part in the attack and we were fearfully intrigued to hear how they got on.

They are huge prehistoric peeps. They are shaped like an egg with one of the sides, the side which rests on the ground, rather flattened. They are about half the length of a tennis lawn, are heavily armoured enough to resist the splinters of 77 mm and shrapnel, hold ten men inside and one 120-horse-power motor. They go about two-and-a-half miles or less an hour, and will walk through any wall, palings or barrier of wire; they can go through almost any pond and can climb trees, or very nearly so. Anyhow they sort of rear themselves up at it and sort of bend it over and crawl over it. They are armed with a machine gun in front and rear and a six pounder on each side and are very alarming monsters indeed when they condescend to get a move on. Yesterday there were quite a number of them in the attack but they didn't all start. However a few of them got on.

Amongst the prisoners we took were three Commanders of Bavarian Regiments. These conveyed their notions of the show to us afterwards in no guarded terms at all. They described the ferocious and intense bombardment that we put up behind their front line through which they could not retire. When our men were on them they, the Huns, started to line the parapet, when to their horror they perceived these huge, enormous, clumsy, weird prehistoric peeps bearing down on them. Officers yelled to their machine gun companies to pour an intense fire on them whereupon the great megalosaurus-looking beast turned itself towards the machine guns and slowly trod them underfoot. The poor old Boches were horribly frightened.

It was reported that one of them had got to the North East corner of Bouleaux Wood and that three of them were seen entering Flers. We simply could not believe it. We did not know the advance could have gone on so quickly. Then the next wire said that one of the tanks was seen going through High Street, Flers, followed by large crowds of our troops cheering wildly. It must have been fun. . . .

17 September. I suppose you have all been very excited with our advances here. It is good, isn't it? And this morning my telegram from Headquarters says that we have captured 160 officers and 3900 other ranks and six guns, while our casualties are not heavy. But I have heard nothing of Charlie Feversham or Harry Lascelles. . . .

I am pinning on to this a little drawing that Fuller made

of one of the new prehistoric centipedes. You will see that it has a Hotchkiss gun on the roof and a six pounder and a machine gun on each side, a very formidable affair indeed. But they went too slow, everyone says. It is not that they cannot manage to surmount obstacles of all kinds, but the ground is so frightfully pitted with shell holes that even with the length of the centipedes they do not get a fair purchase. Consequently they only get along very slowly indeed.

The troops marched behind them patting them on the rear end of the armour-plating and prodding them with their bayonets to get them along. It caused great amusement and enthusiasm amongst the men who never paid any attention to shells or bullets at all. . . .

21 September. There is no news at all. This terrible weather has quite put a lid on the fighting for the present and now that the days get so short and the nights so long and cold, you may really say that the close season for fighting is on us. . . .

22 September. I meant to have written and told you yesterday that Harry Lascelles has again been wounded. He was hit as you will see in his note and now is for three months in Blighty. The Guards Division lost very heavily on account of the Regular Division, one of the original Expeditionary Force Divisions, hardly moving on their right. This was an immense contrast to the brand new Division in which Charlie Feversham is commanding a Battalion on the left of Harry's Division, who went on, through and past everything right into Flers. . . .

I cannot write any longer in a chatty strain. General Lyon has just telephoned to me that poor Charlie Feversham has been killed. I was afraid to ask yesterday. I could not believe that both he and Harry would come through, but bitterly as I would have regretted Harry's death, Charlie's affects me even more. Poor dear fellow. I only saw him, thank God, a few short days ago and I longed for him to get out of this show without a hurt. I prayed that he might not be killed in this damnable war. I can't bear to think of it nor of his poor dear Queenie and kiddies. My heart is really too full to write. I really loved Charlie, and his last letter to me was so sweet. You have got it, haven't you?

General Lyon was so kind. He did not want me to see it in the wireless-press without warning. He told me he had bad news, but I did not know it was so bad. Thank Heaven I am going to see you soon for I feel thoroughly depressed with the news. I will write to Queenie, but I don't know what to say, for I feel too sorry for her to be able to say anything almost. . . .

24 September. . . . Poor Charlie's photograph in the papers made me feel so wretched. And the short biography reads so cold and so inadequate beside the human being one knew. All that sophistry about being the death he would have liked best is so awful. Nobody wants to die at all, and this blasted war is killing everybody. . . .

28 September. . . . You may expect me on Tuesday about nine o'clock or so. . . .

29 September. . . . Tomorrow is the last day of September and soon the leaves will begin to turn their colour and say goodbye to the branches where the breezes have shaken and blown them about since April; so that perhaps they will be pleased to turn golden and brown and flutter gently and tenderly down to rest in the soft damp grass. This is a poetic way of looking at the autumn leaves, but our soldiers will never appreciate damp grass in October. It will not do them any good at all and I question very much in a country

absolutely billet-less, with all the villages in dust and ruins, all the water supply destroyed, all the fields a mass of shell pits, whether real fighting can go on during the winter. I suppose somehow or other it will have to do so, for we cannot afford to let the Boche dig himself in again and make his position impregnable almost, like he has done during the last two winters.

Almost the biggest question of the moment to my mind is 'Is she going to meet me at the Station?' Or 'Am I going to find her at the Ritz?' I am now having a bet with myself and it is three to one bar one, perhaps even more.

I have a letter this morning from Potter telling me about poor Charlie's death. He did splendidly, a more gallant man never walked. I will show you the letter at home. At home! Doesn't it sound almost too glorious to think of?

When Ward-Jackson returned home for good, in February 1918, it was to channel his pent-up energies into public service rather than private pleasures. He had once before stood for Parliament, unsuccessfully, at South Manchester in 1910 (largely on a Unionist platform). He had no trouble with the Leominster Division in Herefordshire. Of his four years in the House of Commons The Times *obituarist wrote that he was 'much beloved', but added: 'It is to be doubted whether his heart was ever in politics. While a member, however, he threw all his energy and enthusiasm into the representation of his constituency.'*

The Ward-Jacksons moved from palatial Shobden to comparatively modest Street Court near Leominster. With financial problems beginning to rear their head, Queenie later turned her business abilities to the running of what William Ward-Jackson describes as 'an elaborate, very luxurious chicken farm'. But Charlie remained the generous host. One can imagine that round his table would have gathered many of those mentioned in the letters who had been fellow brass hats during the war, doubtless reminiscing nostalgically over the port and brandy about the bad old days on the Western Front.

However, in the autumn of 1916 the war was still a grim reality. Back from leave Ward-Jackson resumed the daily letters to Queenie that were to continue for the next fourteen months. The bloody and inconclusive Battle of the Somme was drawing to a close: on the VII Corps' sector of the front evidently with a bang rather than a whimper.

Ward-Jackson's letter of 16 November, the day the history books record as the final day of the battle, is newsy and buoyant as usual. Like all the rest of his letters it bears the stamp of a man who, for all his background of sybaritic privilege, retained a consuming curiosity in all that was going on around him and a warm regard for his fellow-men: in this case men of the Royal Naval Division, heroes of Gallipoli, now making their debut on the Western Front.

There was a great bombardment yesterday as I told you, and Pakenham and I rode out to our favourite place about four miles off to have a look. But it was very hazy and one could see no distance at all – not a scrap of Germany. I have just had another report in and see that we got thirteen officers and five hundred men prisoners yesterday and the total now is 5678. It is bitterly cold and was frosty last night.

It is very amusing to hear everybody laugh at the RND. They say they all had a spit into the ditch and hitched up their trousers before they went over. And signalled 'All's well' from the focsle head when they got into the Boche front line. I would like to see some of them very much and hear what they have to say about it. . . .

Chapter 5

Churchill's War Babies P73

Six weeks after the outbreak of the First World War, the revelation that cadets of only fifteen had been distributed among the battleships and cruisers of the Royal Navy for active service at sea caused an outcry in Parliament and the press.

'Children who can do no possible good on board our men-of-war in time of action' was how one MP described them, following news that a number of midshipmen, aged from fifteen to sixteen and a half, had been among the 1400 drowned when the cruisers Aboukir, Hogue *and* Cressy *were torpedoed and sunk by a German U-boat while on patrol in Home waters.*

The issue was one that brought dramatically to light the feelings of those most emotionally involved: the mothers of those 'children'. In a letter to the Morning Post *on 30 September 1914, 'the Mother of a Dartmouth cadet' passionately rebuked the MP for 'a most cruel and gratuitous insult to those gallant boys of whom we, their mothers, and, I venture to think, the whole British nation are justly proud.'*

'For my own part' she went on 'if my son can best serve England at this juncture by giving his life for her, I would not lift one finger to bring him home. If any act or word of mine should interfere with or take from him his grandest privilege, I could never look him in the face again.'

The letters that follow were written to his mother, father and

129

sister by one such cadet. They are all now dead, and there is no knowing what were the feelings of the mother of Midshipman Leslie Berridge as she awaited news of her son in the heat of battle off Gallipoli, as other mothers of her class waited to learn the latest escapades of sons with two or three years of boarding-school life still ahead of them.

To later generations the 'death and glory' patriotism that could so override a mother's natural instincts is difficult to imagine. But that it was no passing phase is clear from a book published nearly two years after the start of the war. Entitled From Dartmouth to the Dardanelles, it comprised the log of a midshipman, edited by his mother.

In her foreword and linking passages the mother employs all those resounding phrases and euphemisms that strike such a hollow note today but were then fraught with meaning. Death is 'the Great Deliverer', 'a mighty and glorious Angel, setting on the brow the crown of immortality.' Of the Dartmouth cadets at Gallipoli she writes: 'They gave all they had – their health and their youth, and in some cases their lives, and I think the names of all these "children" are written in letters of flame on the Roll of England's Honour – England's Glory.'

No high-sounding phrases embellish the boyishly extrovert letters to his parents scrawled by Midshipman Berridge from the battleship Albion. But that patriotism, loyalty, dedication and devotion to duty were so ingrained in him as to be taken for granted can be deduced from the testimony of a fellow-cadet who shared his early training and knew him well.

Captain Eric Bush has written his own account of those days in his autobiographical Bless Our Ship and his authoritative Gallipoli (published in 1975). His recollections have been invaluable in setting the background and filling in details for a collection of letters which, though unique of their kind, are for the most part tantalisingly uncommunicative.

'For two years at the Royal Naval College, Osborne, from the age of twelve-and-a-half, I slept in the bunk next to Berridge' Captain Bush recalls. 'That was because dormitories were arranged alphabetically for the 450 cadets, who were organised in six Terms, named after famous Admirals. We were in the Blake Term.

'We were all the sons of middle-class professional men and had been to prep schools. I never became a close friend of Berridge. I found him a bit cocky, perhaps because he was a fast developer and I was a slow developer. He struck me as rather pleased with himself, rather superior.

'What we shared was complete loyalty to our Term and dedication to the great traditions of the Royal Navy. There were only two "desertions" while I was at Osborne, when two cadets rowed a boat across the Solent to the mainland and tried to get home. One was withdrawn from the College by his parents, the other was publicly flogged. It was a ceremonious occasion, with the whole college formed up into a square. The offence was read out, he was bent over a gymnasium "horse" and made to grasp a broom handle. He was awarded twelve cuts. He stuck it to number eight, then yelled the place down.

'Corporal punishment was accepted by us as part of our character-training even when we were serving aboard warships during the war. I knew of one midshipman being awarded cuts for some misdemeanour shortly after he had been awarded the DSC. The traditions of the Navy were all-important to us and it would never have entered our minds to challenge them.'

In peacetime the two years at Osborne would have been followed by two further years at Dartmouth and six months at sea in a training cruiser before a cadet was finally appointed to the Fleet as midshipman at about seventeen-and-a-half. For Berridge, Bush and their fellow-cadets, fate – and Winston Churchill – decreed otherwise.

Half way through their first (and only) term at Dartmouth, in the summer of 1914, Churchill, as First Lord of the Admiralty, came to inspect them. Their potential officer-like qualities must have impressed him. On 1 August, three days before the

131

declaration of war, the order came to mobilise.

*The 434 cadets thus pitchforked into the war became popu-
larly known as 'Winston Churchill's War Babies'. Aboard the
ships on the Second Fleet among which they were distributed (in
the confident belief that they could continue their training there
in comparative safety) they went by other names: 'snotties',
'warts', Commander's 'doggies', Navigator's 'tankeys'.*

*It is this kind of language, mixed with schoolboy slang, that
Berridge uses. His sixty-three letters are an amalgam of high
spirits and deference, impetuosity and obedience, worldly
wisdom and naïvety. In the first two one can immediately
discern the 'cockiness' to which Captain Bush refers:*

1 August 1914. RNC Dartmouth.

Dear Mother and Father,

I may not be able to come back at the appointed time as
cadets at Dartmouth mobilise for war. On Tuesday evening
the skipper gave us a jaw telling us that when the order to
mobilise came we were all to get out of the college with our
chests in 5 hours from that time. Blake and Grenville go by
first train to Chatham. I am on the Albion. Of course the
trains are specials and there are 5, 1 to Chatham, 1 to Sheerness and 1 to Devenport. Of course everybody is living
waiting every minute for the order 'mobilise'. It rather
interferes with exams but all the same it's rather fun. I've
done jolly well so far in the exams. Thanks awfully for the
5/-. Please can you let Miss Friend know that I don't get
time to write.

Best love from your loving Leslie.

Later. We are now in the train on our way to Chatham to
embark in our ships. For goodness sake don't be nervous,
it's a rotten show. We won't get any fighting at all only do
coast defence in the leakiest and most aged barge in the
service.

We did some smart work on getting out of the college. The order 'mobilise' was given at 4 p.m. The chests were packed hauled out of the dormitory and shoved on carts within an hour, we then had our travelling money given out and had tea. We left the college exactly 2 hours after the order mobilise. It took some time to get the train off.

I must stop now. Don't be nervous.

Best love from your loving Leslie.

4 August. I told you about the way we got out of the college busting half the chests by the way. When we arrived at Chatham we discovered that our ship wasn't there so were marched to the barracks where we slept in the gymn on the floor. We spent Sunday there and by the evening were sick of it. We may not give our position or our movements to anyone and to prevent tell-tale postmarks all letters go to London GPO and are thence distributed. I hear a rumour that England has at last declared war.

I am afraid there are very few things to say. Thanks for your letter. Love to Leila.

To a military historian Berridge's letters would be of value only for the descriptions of Albion's *part in the Allied naval attack on the Turkish forts guarding the Dardanelles in February and March 1915 and in the Gallipoli landings a month later. For the purposes of this book the interest lies in the glimpses they give of a boy in love with the idea of war, its alarms and excursions, death and glory.*

Berridge was no born letter-writer. Most of his letters are brief and nearly all end with get-away excuses like 'This is all I have time for now' or 'I must stop now as the mail will go soon' (there are recurrent excuses for not having written to Miss

*ho was his governess before Osborne). But there is
...et a clear enough picture of a boy thirsting for adven-*

*Captain Bush recalls that a very popular serial in the peri-
odical* Chums *before the war had been 'The Defence of the
Motherland' by Captain Frank Shaw, illustrated with pictures
of destroyers 'dashing about, blazing away at each other and
firing torpedoes'. That was the kind of thing Berridge no doubt
hankered for, and, though denied encounters with enemy warships, he was to find excitement enough.*

*Though youth is the theme of this chapter it should be remem-
bered that in the navy itself at that time there was nothing in the
least remarkable about the presence of boys aboard a warship.
'Ships' boys', or boy ratings, had for long been an integral part
of a crew and during the war far outnumbered 'Churchill's war
babies' (Captain Bush estimates that there were some forty
ships' boys aboard the cruiser on which he served compared with
ten midshipmen).*

*While Captain Bush recalls being on friendly terms with a
number of boy ratings, and playing football against them, there
is mention of only one in Berridge's letters (then only because he
had died and been buried at sea). That they were taken for
granted, in much the same way as domestic servants were taken
for granted back home, is indicated by a reference made by the
midshipman's mother who edited* From Dartmouth to the
Dardanelles.

*Looking back to the controversy over the mobilisation of
cadets, she writes: 'Did those who agitated for these Cadets to
be removed from the post of danger forget, or did they never
realise, that on every battleship there is a large number of boys,
sons of the working classes, whose service is indispensable? It
seemed to me that if my son was too young to be exposed to such
danger, the principle must apply equally to the son of my cook,
or my butcher, or my gardener, whose boys were no less precious
to them than mine was to me.'*

Aboard the antiquated battleship Albion, *in which he had been so chagrined to find himself, Berridge at least saw something of the world before going into action in the Dardanelles. On escort and patrol duties she sailed to Gibraltar, the Cape Verde islands, South Africa, Ascension, St Helena and through the Suez Canal to the Mediterranean. During these seven months his parents and sister Leila had to content themselves with eight mostly brief letters, each concluding with an imperative 'I must stop now,' from which these are extracts:*

[Undated, but evidently in September 1914 off the Spanish coast.] The Spanish papers issued a lovely report that His Majesty's Ship *Albion* had been sunk with all hands just because they heard us firing at battle practice. I was in the fore turret when we were firing. The noise inside is not in the form of a bang but the whole turret shakes and rings like a huge gong. I was sitting just behind the left gun. First we fired ¾ charge and the gun came back quite slowly, but full charge was appalling, the gun came back at the run. I don't think this is prohibitied news as it does not give away the position or state of the ship.

The ship has just bought a small kid for a pet. When it becomes a goat there will probably be ructions. The commander bought it I believe. It is a ripping little animal. We have played deck-hockey a lot lately but only in the evenings. I wish I could tell you all the things that have happened up to the present time but it is prohibited. . . .

3 October. I have been told that this is a legitimate story so I am going to tell it to you. One morning of a certain day of a certain month I was down below writing my journal when suddenly someone yelled that the navigator wanted his 'tankey' (that is me) so I rushed up above on to the bridge. On arrival he presented me with his cigarette case and told

135

me to fill it as if we were going to fight he must smoke.

This gave me rather a shock but I went and filled it and brought it back and then heard that there were two ships of war on the starboard bow a long way away. Soon I made them out and heard various people remarking that they were large cruisers. I was sent for a fighting ship photograph book but they didn't find any clue as to their nationality there and their colours were indiscernible.

The captain then had 'Down windsails' piped. Windsails are canvas funnels with a wind catch at the top to convey air below. This was the first step in clearing for action. A few minutes later, the boats being flooded to prevent fire, the 'Action' was sounded off. All rails were released and laid flat and various temporary awnings were stowed away, then everyone went to his station and cleared away the guns.

The captain, the navigator and myself were the only ones now on the bridge. After some time the signalmen reported that they were hoisting their colours which were presently made out to be —. This nation is neutral so that we had no chance of a scrap. The 'secure' was sounded and according to after accounts the language used by the men was not fit for the drawing room. . . .

PS. Have you heard that Holt, Gore Brown, Stubbs and others to the number of eight have been drowned in the *Hogue*, *Aboukir* and *Cressy* disaster? Will you please write to Miss Friend and thank her etc. as I find it very hard to get time and writing materials to write to anyone but you.

26 December. . . . It might interest you to know that we are quite happy here and have plenty of amusement in fishing and sticking lumps of putty with flags in them on other snotties' noses whilst asleep. When on the Cape station we had a very fine time going to picnics and landing for amusement every other day or so.

Pardon the pencil but Maclean has just sharked my pen and as he is going to write up his log I have very kindly let him keep it. – !!!!!!! Pardon the language but some one charged me. . . .

7 January 1915. I have just got piles of letters so I'll try to answer the questions in them. Firstly, Sammy Stone is an appalling ass and rather inclined to sulk. Secondly cinemas don't grow in *Albions* – it's bad for them. In other words we haven't got one. It is only the later ships that have them for the purpose of keeping the hands as much as possible from going ashore and getting drunk. Thirdly I can think of no clothes I want now. I have got tons of summer things and 3 suits of whites. I haven't been very extravagant so far and excluding the clothes and photographic gear which I have bought I haven't to the best of my knowledge exceeded the amount you thought enough. I am sending a little inlaid box and a scarf for Mother and a blue scarf for Leila in the same packet. I will send something to father when I can think of something appropriate so don't please feel left out of it. . . .

4 February. Yesterday we were steaming along and suddenly sighted a submarine, at least it looked like one, so sheered off a short way and then resumed our course. It really was very like one but really it was a target. . . .

The other day one of the ships boys died of an awful kind of abscess which swelled his face horribly and was given a burial at sea. It is really horrible to think that any should die other than those actually fighting as to die in action must be far better.

I do hope we come right home soon and get leave and then perhaps commission a new ship. Wouldn't it be fine in the *Royal Oak* or one of those other new 15 inchers. I am afraid there are no more news, so I must stop.

137

10 February. . . . Father is correct in his supposition that we were in the sanitorium not because of illness but because the ship was in —. Whilst up there we were most energetic and climbed Mount Sinai or Spurious Peak of Burg or something in spite of the snakes which are reported to live on the hills. We saw one one day. It was very small and very frightened because it simply glided in a thin wriggly line across the path. It wasn't a puff adder because it was only about 1″ thick and 1½ to 2 feet long and black. We all had sticks. . . .

We've just subscribed 10 bob each to a gramophone for the gun-room. Corlett sat on two records the 3rd day of our possession. We are going to get some more at our next Port. . . .

PS. Auntie Tottie offered me Tango for a pet, could you please tell her that even if the commander let us have him he couldn't be given proper attention. By the way the goat died for some reason and had to be dropped overboard.

Six days later Berridge at last had something to write home about. The naval attack on the Dardanelles had begun and Albion, *that 'leakiest and most aged barge in the service', had been gloriously transformed into a fighting man-o'-war, thundering broadsides with the best of them. His baptism by fire had come.*

This gallant attempt by British and French warships to silence the Turkish guns guarding the Dardanelles and the narrow entrance into the Sea of Marmara might have led to the capture of Constantinople, the opening up of the Black Sea to Allied shipping to and from Russia, and a speeding up of final victory. That it was called off, when success seemed within sight on 18 March, and that the bloodbath of Gallipoli ensued,

138

has been a matter of controversy for historians. What is indisputable is that it was an unprecedented action (warships against artillery) of which the navy could be proud. To Berridge it was 'a splendid time'.

The straits of the Dardanelles (the ancient Hellespont), forty miles long and from less than a mile to four miles wide, which divide Europe from Asia, were defended on both sides by Turkish forts mounting a total of 150 guns, the most modern with a range of 15,000 yards. To silence them, particularly in the channel known as the Narrows, which runs into the Sea of Marmara, and to go on to clear the minefields, the greatest concentration of naval strength that had ever been seen in the Mediterranean had been assembled.

The first, and least perilous, phase of the attack, the reduction of the outer forts at the entrance to the straits, in which eight British and four French battleships took part, began on 19 February. For censorship reasons (apart from his natural reluctance to put pen to paper) it was four days later that Berridge wrote a letter beginning: 'We are having a splendid time now no one thinks of any danger to himself the enemy's firing is too rotten. I can't tell you anything much that we've done or are going to do. . . .'

It is not until 4 March that he gets off a three-page letter, together with a chart of the Dardanelles he has drawn, marking the forts attacked by Albion *and with sketches of how they appeared humping out of the coastline.*

I can give you some really interesting news now. We are off the Dardanelles and have been in action four or five times. I won't give you too detailed an account of what we've done as I should then have nothing to tell you when I come home. But anyway if you would like to come and see me I will have great pleasure in meeting you in Constantinople in a few months

139

The first day of proper action we went in to finish off the actual guns of the forts (from 3000 yards) the breastworks of which had already been badly knocked about by long-range fire from the bigger ships. We met with no opposition and started firing on No. 4 fort (see chart). The right gun was already lying down. After some few shots we began to hit and soon dismantled the left gun. We then turned round and fired the port 6″ at No. 6 fort (see chart). Our shooting was again good and we soon began to hit the guns and embrasures.

When satisfied with the effects of our firing we started out again but had first to go astern to get away from a shoal in doing which we rammed our stern into a mine field (the mines are fired from observing places on shore) and one exploded on our port bow. After which some silly little splashes started all round (causing an exit from the bridge of the Captain, Navigator and self) probably from small field guns accompanied by a whiz. The Admiral made a signal to us: 'You have been shooting very well, Congratulate you.'

The next day, 26th of Feb. we went in to about 12,000 yards from No. 8 fort and fired 12″ at it. The first 3 were short but after some hints from an aeroplane we began to hit and kept it up well. At times some large splashes appeared quite near us but the guns that made them were not located. The splashes were treated with contempt and we went on firing for some time. But the Turks got our range and nearly hit us so we went on and turned round (we had been stopped). At one time shots were falling all round us but we came out untouched.

Our next dose was on Monday the 1st of March. We intended to shell No. 8 fort again but just before we opened fire shot began to fall unpleasantly close so we had to move on so as to keep their shots falling clear owing to our speed. We then started a sort of run and turned round in 2

140

complete circles. In the second run, instead of a whiz –
splash, there was a whiz . . . bang and we were hit on the
fo'c'sle and again twice aft, one causing splinter wounds to
5 men. We were then ordered to draw off a little and that
finished our bit for the day.

The objection to this game is that the batteries on shore
can see us but we have to look for them and unless we
actually hit the gun we only drive the men away for a time.

I must stop now,

Best love from your loving Leslie.

*That Berridge was in a relatively communicative mood now
that something was happening is evidenced by the fact that he at
last got down to writing to Miss Friend, who by now would
have had a number of messages passed on to her by his parents
regretting he had so little time to spare for letters. Dated 11
March, it is the only letter in the collection not to his parents and
sister.*

We are having plenty of fun from Turkish shells, but we
are rarely in danger of being hurt as their gunnery is the
poorest show imaginable. They managed to hit us one day
in about 6 places, wounding 5 men, but it wasn't their
fault! Some of their efforts are really painful, I have often
seen shots fall about a mile away from any ship.

It may surprise you to hear that we are allowed to smoke
in action and I find it very soothing when you can hear
shells whistling close overhead and falling a few yards clear.
One day we had them badly when some 6″ howitzers
opened up on us. Splashes fell about 5 yards clear, 2 on the
starboard bow, one on the port bow and some were even
astern. The splashes these shells make are colossal and

141

occasionally are higher than the tallest masts in the Squadron which is about 150 feet.

Best love, Leslie.

All of this was in the nature of a dress rehearsal for the great day, 18 March, the day of the attack on the Narrows. A thin strip of deep water, five miles long and less than a mile wide, bristling on either side with the guns of eight major Turkish batteries, this was the gateway to Constantinople.

Accompanied by cruisers, destroyers and minesweepers, twelve British and four French battleships were engaged, in three divisions, under the command of Admiral de Robeck aboard the flagship Queen Elizabeth. Albion *was in the third division of six battleships, held in reserve. The plan was to so batter the forts at the Narrows during the day that minesweepers would be enabled to clear a channel during the evening, through which the battleships could pass next morning into the Sea of Marmara.*

Berridge's account of that memorable day, partly copied from his log, is scarcely one that would have passed muster among the readers of Chums. *There is no indication of the romantic setting, near the plain of ancient Troy, of the brilliant sun shining down on a calm sea. There is little evocation of the heat of action later, with (as Alan Moorehead describes it in* Gallipoli) *'the forts enveloped in clouds of dust and smoke, with an occasional flame spurting out of the debris, the ships slowly moving through a sea pitted with innumerable fountains of water, and sometimes disappearing altogether in the fumes and spray, the stabs of light from the howitzers firing from the hills, and the vast earthquake rumbling of the guns.'*

But perhaps more moving in its way is the picture one gets of a fifteen-year-old boy gritting his teeth before action, and cool-headed during it. His first letter is evidently written shortly after the action had commenced, at 10.30 am, with the first ten bat-

142

tleships entering the straits to run the gauntlet of the shore guns as they steamed towards the Narrows.

18 March. We are now embarking on the most dangerous part of the bombardment which of course is reducing the Narrows. The first Division and four Frenchmen have already started and after four hours under fire they (the French) are relieved by us and 3 others. I have put most of my gear below the waterline in case a 14 inch or something comes into the gun room.

I will write some more rot in action so as to keep my mind occupied.

Once we've knocked those forts out we will be all right and the next bit of amusement will be hunting down the Turkish fleet.

I must stop now as soon we will be getting under weigh to proceed to death or glory. What!

Berridge found no time to write 'more rot' during the harrowing action in which Albion *was engaged that afternoon. And his letter next day is terse.*

19 March. It turned out that I didn't go to death and I don't know whether I covered myself with glory either. I made rather an ass of myself on the whole because when we got out again I reported the barometer smashed, which of course was rather a minor detail after what had happened.

The extraordinary part was that practically no *shots* did any damage and we landed ours in the forts with extraordinary accuracy.

I'm sending some Maltese lace and some more photos in a book. Please if possible keep them in the same order. In case we are sunk I will send off various things which I don't want. I always wear my waistcoat so I'm quite safe.

For a boy who had just witnessed the sinking of a battleship and the crippling of two others, this was in the best traditions of the Silent Service, even allowing for the dictates of the censor. Berridge's next letter was written on 25 March.

I still can't tell you of the last and most desperate of our attacks. As soon as I can I'll send a long account which I will write in the meantime. . . .

Please don't get anxious if you see stories of the dangers we get in and out of because most of them are very largely exaggerated. There will probably be an account in some paper of our point of view of the show as two reporters came on board one day (night rather) and left in the morning probably full of stuffing which was put into them by the wardroom. By stuffing I don't mean breakfast, I mean journalistic substance. I really think that they are rather enterprising fellows living out here and getting news home, goodness knows how. . . .

Berridge's 'long account' followed a few days later, with a detailed chart showing the movements of Albion *and her sister-ships during the attack on the Narrows.*

I am afraid I can never give you a sufficiently vivid account of the 18th of March to impress you with the horror of some parts of it. Anyway this is my best taken direct from my log. . . .

At 1.25 our division entered the Dardanelles and stopped

just inside awaiting the order to relieve the French ships. Whilst we were waiting the first tragedy occurred. The *Bouvet*, which was returning at a good speed close to the southern shore was suddenly seen to list to starboard and as we watched she turned slowly over and, still moving along at a good speed, sank out of sight.

As she went over thick columns of smoke poured out of her funnels across the water. Picket boats and the flanking ship were on the scene at once and destroyers were ordered to close. How many were picked up I don't know. The destroyers were outside so arrived very late. The actual time of this was about 1.56 and the whole was over in 2 minutes.

At 2.14 we were ordered to proceed up to the line at 1½ knots and the four relieving ships went ahead, passing through the line of big ships at 2.31, being ourselves passed by the destroyers rushing to the scene of the disaster. The howitzer battery was already busy firing at them. At 2.37 we reduced speed so as just to stem the current about 1 mile ahead of the big ships and at 2.40 we opened fire on our fort, the others doing ditto with theirs. (Here I leave a lot of more or less uninteresting stuff out.)

At 3.34 we were ordered to extend our distance from the enemy which we did ahead as we were heading the other way and firing our after-turret whilst the other 3 went astern. This was the *Irrisistible*'s undoing and she struck a mine aft and heeled over.

Here comes about the most splendid part of it. I dare say you've read accounts of the calmness with which the *Hogue*'s people waited for the final plunge. This was different, field batteries at once got the range of her (she was stopped) and were straddling her every time. And all through it her people were waiting quietly for the destroyers to take them off. One shot fell right in the middle of the quarter deck and must have wrought awful havoc. But

145

there was no panic, no one tried to get away before ordered to.

And the destroyers. They were wonderfully handled and saved the situation completely. Without them the job of getting off the men would have been very slow. The *Ocean* [one of the battleships in Berridge's division] was ordered to stand by to take her in tow. (I will now go on without my log leaving times out). We opened a rapid fire on batteries on the southern shore which were still firing on the *Irresistible* (about 50 men were left on board to work on the fo'c'sle if taken in tow).

Later the *Ocean* was told to take her in tow as she was only settling very very slowly. The *Ocean* went up to her and stayed there some time whilst destroyers passed between the two ships. It was naturally presumed that towing hawsers were being passed across but soon the *Ocean* (whose wireless had broken down) started to go astern and when she'd come some way down she turned and was seen to have a list to starboard and a fire in the region of her engine room.

Destroyers at once closed on her and took all her people off and then left her. Unfortunately the *Irresistible* was in a part where there was no current so she didn't float out of range and what was really happening whilst the *Ocean* was up by her was that the working party was being taken off.

These sketches give my impression of the three ill-fated ships as I last saw them. Of other damage to the fleet I will not tell but the day was far from a victory for us. Something near our fort exploded and burst violently and I believe most of the forts stopped firing but the guns were probably intact and the Turks merely left temporarily.

I hope the next show will be better.

Best love from Leslie

There was to be no 'next show' in the Dardanelles. But Berridge's assumption that the outcome of the day's action amounted to a defeat remains arguable. That night Commodore Roger Keyes, Chief of Staff, returned in a destroyer to see what had happened to the crippled Irresistible *and* Ocean, *and what he found convinced him that victory could be in the offing.*

In the silent and eerie aftermath of battle, Turkish searchlights swept the dark waters. There was no sign of the two battleships. They had by now sunk and lay out of the enemy's reach, safely at the bottom in deep water. But more important to him than that was the fact that, apart from the searchlights, there seemed no sign of life on either shore.

'I had,' he wrote later, 'a most indelible impression that we were in the presence of a beaten foe. I thought he was beaten at 2 p.m. I knew he was beaten at 4 p.m. And at midnight I knew with still greater certainty that he was absolutely beaten. It only remained for us to organise a proper sweeping force and devise some means of dealing with the drifting mines to reap the fruits of our efforts.'

In the event the fleet was withdrawn, to make its next appearance in a subsidiary role. It was now up to the army to come to grips with the enemy, storming the beaches of the Gallipoli peninsula.

Berridge's limitations as a letter-writer (later to be commented on by Albion's *senior officer) are nowhere more evident than during the initial phase of the Gallipoli campaign. On 25 April he was an eye-witness to the landings on 'V' beach, one of the most dramatic and gallant exploits of the war. Though censorship has always to be reckoned with, it seems incredible that in his next three letters home there is not even the vaguest hint of this. It is not until 22 May, a month after the event, that he unbuttons: 'Of course you have heard about the landing of troops on the peninsula. I will tell you our experiences . . .'.*

In the naval bombardment that preceded the Gallipoli landings at daybreak on 25 April, Albion *had been allotted the*

147

most important of the southern beaches, 'V' beach near the ruined fort of Sedd-el-Bahr. This was the beach where a 'Trojan horse' was employed to surprise the enemy, in the shape of an old collier, The River Clyde. *While men of the Royal Dublin Fusiliers leapt ashore from a flotilla of ships' boats, the collier was run aground to disgorge men of the Royal Munster Fusiliers.*

This was the beach where Midshipmen Drewry and Malleson (both in their late teens) and Able Seamen Samson and Williams, assisting in the landings, were subsequently awarded the VC for valour. And it was above this beach on the following day (as witnessed by Berridge) that Colonel Doughty-Wylie and Captain Walford led a spectacular charge to capture the fort, subsequently to be awarded posthumous VCs.

Rarely can a boy of fifteen have gazed upon such scenes of courage and carnage: and at least something of excitement and awe comes over in his belated account.

. . . I was called at about 4.30 a.m. and got on the bridge in a few minutes. The dawn was just coming and as the light strengthened we could see two ships ahead already inside. Just before 5 a.m. we anchored off Sedd-el-Bahr. All round the end of the peninsula ships were visible anchored close. At 5 a.m. punctually we all opened fire. The next hour or so was filled, every second of it, with the bangings of guns and the whistling noise of their journey through the air.

A beach just round the corner was taken and the troops established themselves along the ridges at the top. For a few minutes, as the first boats got near that beach, they were under a heavy fire but were not stopped.

On our beach a collier, specially lightened in the bows, was to run aground. She was very late and it was almost 6 before she was on the mud and her people started landing and at the same time tows of boats went ashore and landed

148

their men. The slaughter was awful and you could see them falling on the beach and in the water (they had to wade some way). They got into dead ground under a bank, however, and there remained for the whole day.

All the time they landed there was an infernal noise going on. The rattle of maxims and pom-poms and the pinging of rifles going on almost ceaselessly. How the Turks stood our fire I don't know. I don't mind admitting I'd have hopped it full speed. There are rumours that they were chained to their maxims.

Meanwhile troops had been landed all round the end of the peninsula and the beach next to ours had done splendidly and men from it had already got on to the cliffs and had established a signal station on our side of the lighthouse on Cape Helles. As I said, our beach were hung up temporarily but in the night more men were landed ready for the morrow.

The morrow came [26th April] and with it a splendid sight which very few have witnessed. The troops advanced bit by bit up the hill until near the top. It was wonderfully done and I didn't see a man fall all the way. They advanced from cover to cover in rushes. Luckily the ground was good for them so that there was plenty of cover.

They rushed to the top and took an old fort which gave them a splendid position to hold. Just as the final rush was made the main body of our troop landed on our beach came out of the village of Sedd-el-Bahr, miraculously found a way through the barbed wire entanglements, and joined hands with the rest at the top. Of course all this, up to the final rush, had been under cover of our fire which was of a very rapid and exact nature.

Two of these photos are of our beach. Both show the ship ashore, one being bigger than the other. They need slow printing.

This is all I have time for now so I must stop.

149

A final extract from Berridge's letters records one of his diciest experiences, on 23 May, when the Albion *ran aground off the northern sector of the Gallipoli peninsula, 'on a portion of land occupied by Turks and well within rifle range.' There is an element of the comic, as well as the potentially tragic, in this picture of the 'leakiest and most aged barge in the service' being well and truly peppered by Turkish shot and shell as frantic efforts are made to dislodge her.*

Berridge's lengthy account begins by describing how the first efforts to shake her free were made by the entire ship's company, assembled on the upper deck, jumping vigorously up and down while holding heavy weights. Then the battleship Canopus *and two destroyers came to her assistance. The destroyers, secured alongside, went full speed ahead but failed to budge her. It was now up to the* Canopus *to tow her off.*

. . . The first tow was a failure as the hawser parted. She passed us another hawser and started again. This time she did not bust the thing. At precisely 6.51 a.m. she went ahead, and at 7.7 the enemy fired their first shot.

The first one was miles over but they gradually drew nearer. They soon began to burst the shrapnel over the quarter deck but there was no one there. They tired of this and at 8.15 started to hit us with common shell. Almost every shot hit and every few seconds there was an explosion and the clattering of falling splinters. One shell set the 12-pounder cordite on fire on the port side of the shelter deck.

At 9.11 we got off, being roughly 1 hour under fire. Our total casualties were 1 killed and 9 or 10 wounded. Cheap wasn't it? On leaving we cheered the *Canopus* like blazes and she returned it. I expect we'll be good friends in future. We must have been hit anything up to 100 times, not counting shrapnel with which we are covered. The ship now appears to be in a hopeless condition with funnels like pepper pots and cowls like tea strainers. Only 2 holes were made in our side. We *were* lucky for another hour would have had the heavy batteries on the spot and we'd have been on fire from end to end.

Mother dear! I hope you don't mind, but I smoke in moderation. You will understand what a trying life this is with submarines to add to the charms, so *please* forgive me. It is very soothing. . . .

I do hope Mr Campbell's promotion is not stopped by our unfortunate accident. He had a splendid chance this time. He, by the way, strongly advises Leila not to try and get out here in a Red Cross boat. I don't suppose the Turks are particular who they sink.

Omitted from previous extracts have been other personal references to 'Mr Campbell', who was Lieutenant Commander James Campbell, the navigating officer for whom Berridge acted as assistant (or 'tankey'). In two letters to Berridge's parents Campbell refers to himself as 'sea daddy' to the nine midshipmen aboard, though in the caption to a snapshot of them all grouped proudly around him Berridge prefers the term 'snotties' nurse.'

Somewhat in the manner of a housemaster of a boarding school, Campbell held himself responsible for the progress, behaviour and welfare of his charges. And it is clear that Berridge was the one he thought most highly of.

On 2 April 1915 Berridge writes: 'Mr Campbell has really been awfully good to me. He gave me a watch at Simons Town which unfortunately took to gaining, so at Gibraltar he gave me another awfully nice one. Now he's sent to Malta for a telescope for me. It really makes me feel rather awkward.' And on 13 May: 'Mr Campbell has just given me a gorgeous safety razor (you mustn't write to him about it because he doesn't think anything of it and might not like being written to about it) and I shaved with it this morning. He has asked me to come and stop with him when we get back and he is also going to ask a girl (Bonny Boyes) whom I liked and he loved at Simons Town who is coming to England.'

That these gifts were in appreciation of Berridge's stalwart services as 'tankey' is evident from Campbell's letter to Mrs Berridge in which he writes that 'my good wife has ordered a pair of binoculars for Leslie to show her gratitude for all the help he gave me at Suvla.' Captain Bush recalls that it was not unusual for midshipmen's parents to receive letters from ships' officers about their boys, and that his own parents got 'much comfort and pleasure' from letters from the captain and commander of his cruiser.

Berridge's reference to the girl he met on shore leave is the first indication that his thoughts were not entirely taken up with shipboard life. In his book Gallipoli Captain Bush sums up the midshipman's attitude to sex: 'We were approaching adolescence, and sex was beginning to rear its head, but as we seldom saw girls they were seldom discussed, which gave us peace of mind.'

What seems clear from Captain Bush's recollections today is that the parents of 'Churchill's war babies' at that time need have had none of the concern about their moral welfare that the parents of public school boys were shortly to experience with the publication of Alec Waugh's autobiographical novel, The Loom of Youth. Written shortly after leaving Selborne School, its revelations of liaisons between boys, as an accepted part of boarding-school life, created something of a sensation.

In Berridge's letters there is an evident impatience to bridge the gap between adolescence and manhood. 'I'm now 5ft 7 in my shoes' he writes in one letter 'which must be about 5 ft 6½ in socks and a bit less without them.' That almost shamefaced admission to his mother that he had taken to smoking is followed by an announcement that he has changed from *cigarettes to 'a pipe with mild baccy as you don't get any nicotine that way'. And his navigating officer's gift of a safety razor is a proud acquisition.*

He already had an eye for the girls. Bonny Boyes is more than once mentioned. At Malta he meets 'some very nice people called Manduca (very pretty daughter, hush, not a word).' And while serving off Salonika later in the year he writes: 'We've met some awfully nice Canadian sisters and a lot were on board for tea today: they're an awfully jolly lot.'

In a letter to Berridge's father, on 15 October 1915, Commander Campbell (he had got his promotion despite Albion's 'unfortunate accident') pays a tribute to his 'tankey' that must have more than made up for the paucity of information in his son's own letters home. It refers to the aftermath to new landings at Suvla Bay, on 7 August, when 20,000 fresh troops were poured ashore in an attempt to end the stalemate. Campbell had got Berridge appointed as his Assistant Harbour-Master.

. . . We were kept pretty busy and were on the go day and night (bringing in transports, taking them out, laying down buoys, setting up beacons, surveying the harbour, seeing to the safeguard of the bay). I was very run down with blood poisoning and many times had to let Leslie bring ships in and out of the boom defences and do various other jobs but he never failed me once.

He suits me so well, as although I have a very cheery disposition, I suffer from a quick temper, and then I bite a good deal, but Leslie is never put out and never seems to bear me a grudge, he invariably cheers me up and he is so jolly himself. At the beginning of the war I had an assistant who, if I cursed him in the morning, was useless for the rest of the day – he was so sensitive – but your boy had good grit and judgement, in fact understands me.

We spent 5 weeks at Suvla and I was very proud of the

way Leslie ran my boat. For one so young he is remarkably level headed and steady and is bound to get on. . . . He has such a healthy look and is growing right out of his trousers and is as cheery as possible. . . .

Four months later, off Salonika, Campbell writes a letter to Berridge's mother that can be seen as epitomising the 'Nelson spirit', the bond that held together the crew of a man-of-war, the loyalty and devotion to duty. For him the phrase 'Churchill's war babies' must now have seemed a derisory one. He had seen those Dartmouth cadets tested in action, and was proud, if slightly saddened, by their transformation from boys to 'officers and gentlemen'.

. . . They are all growing up so fast that I am relieved from my post as 'sea-daddy' to them all and they are now under ordinary service routine. None of them realise how I miss looking after them but I can place myself in the position of a parent who has given up everything to get a son on and the son suddenly finds himself able to fly off himself and go out into the world on his own. But still, in a *quiet* way as the senior officer next to the Captain in the ship, I exercise a good deal of authority over them and I always had the boys' interests at heart. Leslie is as loyal as ever and a better mid. I have never known since I have been in the service and I hope thereafter I may have the privilege of doing something for him.

I can't help thinking we will all be home soon and personally I shall be very grateful to anyone who will put their arms round my neck as you suggest in your letter. I am sure my wife won't mind. She knows me too well. I am heartily tired of this bachelor life. My wife is returning to England shortly and you will see her and my two children. . . .

I am awfully pleased with all my boys' progress. They are a real credit to their instructor. I know Leslie has written you recently as I censor all their letters to pick up spelling and punctuation mistakes, though don't find many in Leslie's letters. There is little news from our quarters. We are all alive which is one consulation.

Please thank Leila for her letter. She is a much better correspondent than her brother. I don't write as much as I should, but please remember my interest in your boy never relaxes and you can content your mind that he is everything a gentleman and a good officer should be.

With love,

Yours very sincerely, James Campbell

Berridge's letters were donated to the Imperial War Museum by his sister, Mrs Leila Wilson, in 1968, shortly before her death. When her daughter, Mrs Audrey Robinson, who only dimly remembers her uncle, read them in 1971 she was 'fascinated' and her fifteen-year-old son was 'staggered by them'.

The circumstances of his death, in 1926, seem sadly low key for the aspiring boy cadet Captain Bush knew at Osborne, and the emergent midshipman Commander Campbell saw as on the threshold of a long and distinguished career. His sister Leila wrote briefly about it to the War Museum.

In 1926 he was on the China Station, as Lieutenant in command of H M Submarine L.15. He expected to go home at the end of the year and get married. But in spring his flotilla went to Borneo and Malaya to show the flag. He was killed bathing in Penang – just as they were leaving the pool he ran back to try and do a better backward slide and dive off the chute. So like him really. He died the following morning.

155

Chapter 6

Keeping the Home ~~79|15|1~~
Fires Burning

'Since the big offensive started we hear the guns all day some-times and cannot forget that Ron is there. . . .'

It was the rumbling of the guns on the Somme front that Robert Saunders could hear as he wrote his weekly letter to his eldest son in Canada, on 16 July 1916, from the village of Fletching in the heart of Sussex. All through the war, when a major battle was in progress on the Western Front, and when weather conditions were favourable, that far-off thunder from across the Channel brought home to families in southern England the perils of the trenches, where fathers, husbands, sons, brothers, were undergoing their unimaginable ordeals.

Saunders, headmaster of the village school at Fletching and father of thirteen, was fortunate in that his three sons on active service (Ronald on the Western Front, Robert with the Royal Navy, and Walter with the army in India and Mesopotamia) all survived the war. But for him and his wife Elsie the postman was awaited with as much anxiety as their letters back were awaited with eagerness by their sons – a reassurance that the home fires were still burning and that life went on much as usual.

It is from Saunders' letters to his eldest son William, who had recently emigrated to Canada, that this picture of a middle-class family at war has been pieced together. Usually written in

157

the quiet of a Sunday evening when the rest of the family was at church, they are no doubt typical of the letters that flooded out from homes throughout the country, more concerned with the trivia of family life and local tittle-tattle than with the progress of the war. What they most noticeably (and predictably) seem to lack is any real awareness of what the fighting man was going through.

Frequently commented on in the recollections of First World War combatants has been the emotional gulf between them and the civilian population which they encountered when home on leave. That front-line gunfire in Picardy and Flanders to which Saunders makes periodic reference (from only around seventy miles away as the crow flies) might have come from another world, a world that bore little resemblance to that conjured up for home consumption in the flowery dispatches in newspapers, in government propaganda and patriotic jingoism.

It is necessary to be aware of this dichotomy in reading these letters, which might otherwise seem to make a quite dispropor- tionate fuss about the perils and privations of life on the home front – the spasmodic raids by German zeppelins and bombers, the threat of invasion, rationing and high prices, not to mention the personal ailments which Saunders takes an almost hypo- chondriac zest in recording.

But Saunders was a man of sensibility who, self-admittedly, hid his feelings, and it is possible he was more aware of that dichotomy than the bulk of his letters reveal. An indication of this is the occasion when Ron came home on his first leave from the trenches. Saunders closely watched his son, 'for signs of change', as he sat by the family fireside, and writes: 'It made me feel awfully sad to note many things none of the others would notice in their delight in seeing him.'

When Saunders was appointed headmaster of the Church of England school at Fletching in 1890, with his wife as head of the infants' department, they already had five daughters and one son. During the next twelve years three more daughters and

158

four sons were born. When war broke out they had been married thirty-six years and were looking forward to a well-earned retirement. It is scarcely surprising that, with 250 pupils, aged from five to fourteen, to worry about, quite apart from their own family (five of them still living at home), there is occasional evidence in the letters of friction between Saunders and 'Ma' (though wryly recorded as being in the nature of a family joke).

Fletching was (and still is) an ancient, unspoilt village, largely comprising a straggling High Street that curves round a magnificent thirteenth-century church. The Saunders' home was eighteenth-century St Mary's House opposite the church. The wide, steep-gabled frontage rises directly from the pavement, and the sight of the pretty young Saunders daughters framed in an upper window was one that came to be greatly appreciated by the troops of infantry and cavalry passing through the village from nearby camps.

Behind the roomy house a large kitchen-garden, cultivated by Saunders, looked out over fields to the woods and parkland of Sheffield Park, where Edward Gibbon, a friend of the first Earl of Sheffield, wrote much of The Decline and Fall of Roman Empire (he is buried in Fletching church). The success (or otherwise) of Saunders' fruit and vegetable crops are a recurrent theme in the letters.

It was in the rolling wooded countryside around that Saunders endulged his great passion, nature study. Air-raids apart, the longest and most fluent passages in his somewhat disjointed letters are those describing his nature rambles. He writes with the eye of a Gilbert White about the wild flowers and birds and butterflies, the changing seasons. Assuming he wrote in similar vein to his three sons on active service, such passages would have brought a real breath of the English countryside to the Somme trenches, to a battleship patrolling the North Sea, to the arid hills of the North-West Frontier.

From the 200-page typescript copy of his father's letters made by William Saunders after the war, amounting to over 100,000

159

words, it is here possible to give only representative extracts. To set them in perspective a brief resumé is given of the general situation on the home front during each year of the war. And, as an aid to family references, there follows a list of the eight daughters and five sons (ages in 1914):

Emily ('Em'), 35, married to the headmaster of a London County Council school, who served with the Royal Engineers in France; one daughter.

William John, 33, a chartered accountant in Canada, married Beatrice ('Triss') Weller in 1907; five children.

Annie Winifred ('Win'), 31, married to an LCC schoolmaster, an air-raid warden during the war; three children.

Elsie Mary ('Dic'), married to a cost accountant in 1917, who served as an officer with St John's Ambulance service during the war.

Dorothy Helen ('Nell'), 28, a teacher at a nearby village school.

Edith ('Edi'), 26, helped to keep house for the family.

Louise ('Lu'), 24, joined the WAAC in 1917 and later served in France.

Walter Henry ('Wally'), 21, training as a schoolmaster when mobilized with the Middlesex Regiment, later served in India and Mesopotamia as a Captain in the 6th Ghat Light Infantry.

Robert ('Bob'), 19, served in the Royal Navy throughout the war.

Ronald Frank ('Ron'), 17, served for three years in France with 7th East Surrey Regiment, later commissioned in the Royal West Kents, in 1918 obtained his wings in the RAF.

160

Sarah Kathleen ('Kath'), 15, helped to keep house for the family.

Rosie Francis, died of meningitis aged 14 shortly before the outbreak of war.

Bertram James ('Bert'), 12, attending Uckfield Grammar School, some four miles from Fletching.

When war was declared, on 4 August 1914, the burning issues that divided Britain (notably women's suffrage, Labour unrest and Irish Home Rule) were forgotten and all classes united in opposition to the enemy. Britain's standing army numbered only 750,000 and, from 6 August, the famous poster of a finger-pointing Lord Kitchener ('Your King and Country Need YOU!') opened the floodgates to recruitment.

On 8 August the House of Commons passed the Defence of the Realm Act, which virtually suspended civil rights (known as 'Dora', it was the subject of many a later grouse by Saunders). Press censorship was stringent, and rumours abounded. Invasion seemed a possibility following the bombardment of the north-east coast by German warships in October. Spy-mania was rife, directed particularly at the German communities.

When the first casualty lists began to appear after the retreat from Mons, it became clear that 'victory by Christmas' was out of the question and that Britain might be in for a long war.

Saunders' first letter, on the eve of war, hints at the anticipatory excitement:

2 August. I missed my usual weekly letter last week as I was hardly up to writing. I had a gathering up my nostril which affected my eyes and was so painful I could neither read nor write with comfort. Also Win and family were here and the opportunity to sit down and write quietly was missing.

I did not venture to take Roy or Joan to church in the

morning but Ma, Win, Roy and Joan went in the evening and Joan gave them a lively time. She had been given a penny to put in the bag and took care to inform them during the service she was going to pay for them all. Then she joined in the singing and suddenly smote Roy in the stomach and told him to sing up and at last Win had to bring her home.

Well, we had a fairly lively week but they left yesterday for Portslade, where they are staying for a fortnight and Ma went as far as Lewes with them and went on to Hastings to see about apartments for our holidays. Poor old Bob was coming home for leave but four First Battle Squadrons forming the First Battle Fleet had sudden orders last Wednesday to put to sea with sealed orders and we have heard nothing since and the papers have had orders to publish no information. It has, however, leaked out they were seen steaming at full speed up the North Sea on Friday.

We have been in a great state of excitement as the reservists are being called up, all the railways are guarded, wire entanglements, trench guns, etc., have been hurriedly put round Portsmouth and even our post office has had orders to keep open day and night. Everything points to the Great War, so long expected, being on so you can picture the restless excitement among all classes.

Mr Hood [the vicar] and Doctor have both been in this evening to discuss the situation with me. The Oxo company in which G. Stevenson is, had a wire yesterday to hold all their stock of tinned beef and tongue for the troops, and as far back as two months they were warned to accumulate so our Government has not been caught napping. By the time you get this you will probably know the meaning of it all but everybody recognises how serious it is and the newspapers are eagerly waited for.

Lu and Nell are home for their holiday, and Dic came last night for the bank holiday. She has obtained a post at

Harrow and is looking very well and is in good spirits. Wally is away at camp but we hope he will return on the 8th, though it is just possible he may have to be drafted on some line of communication. . . .

We have continued our dry weather and with the exception of a little rain yesterday are still waiting for the rain that doesn't come. I was digging a celery trench yesterday and as far as I went down there was nothing but dry earth. Mr Fenner says it is the worst year he has had and as hay, corn and roots are so bad he has put in 41,000 cabbages and is now sowing turnips on vacant ground so as to have something. . . .

I can hear them singing the last hymn over at church so I must hurry up to finish before they come. I have still a few minutes as there is a special Intercession for Peace after the service. . . .

8 August. Your letter was a welcome relief from the constant topic of war that is on every one's lips. No one seems able to settle down to work but spends a good part of the time in talking over matters with anyone who comes along. As soon as we are up in the morning we find out at the post office if any has come along, then we wait anxiously for the morning papers which are devoured. Each post is waited for anxiously and any fresh news is passed on to our neighbours.

There has been a very strict censorship on all news so the papers have been supplying us with rumours which are far from satisfying. We don't know yet where our fleets are or whether our army has gone to the continent or not. We have had one letter from Bob who says they didn't know where they were and were forbidden to send the name of any place they would put in to coal. He also said they were at their guns ready for firing at any moment. . . . We have had two postcards from Wally and his regiment (10th

Middlesex) has been sent to Sheerness. He said he had just done four hours' sentry go with ten rounds of ball cartridge.

Poor Mr Fenner was awfully cut up yesterday as they came round and commandeered his black horse Kitty, the one he drove you to the station with. They have been round taking everybody's horses that were suitable and at Uckfield they took the horses out of carriages and carts. As you will see by the papers Kitchener is at the war office and is making his influence felt. I was sorry for Mr Fenner as he was so keen on Kitchener coming to the war office and taking charge of things and it seemed rather rough on him that one of the first results was the loss of his horse of which he was so proud. . . .

Ma is very indignant every time she goes to the grocers or the butchers. Beef is 11d upwards, bacon 1/4 to 1/6, sugar just double etc. We have plenty of plums and apples so shan't have to buy fruit for some time. Thanks to Wally who double-trenched a piece of ground we have a splendid row of beans and I am filling every vacant piece of ground with cabbage and turnip. . . .

Will Muddle caused a little excitement Thursday as he returned home from Eastbourne to don his uniform and join his regiment for Dover. He visited the Griffin and departed on a bike in a very excited state, proclaiming loudly 'well if he got killed he didn't care a damn'. . . .

15 August. . . . Every night there is a rush for the evening papers which arrive at 9 p.m., then doctor and his wife come in to compare notes and discuss the war generally. After they leave Ma generally goes to bed, the girls start to clear supper which has been left owing to one or other coming in late, then I sit to read the news in peace and try to follow the progress of the war from the maps in the papers.

It is, of course, late when we all get to bed and I feel anything but sweet tempered between 4 and 5 a.m. next morning when Ma wakes up and keeps fidgeting and then makes tea. I keep expressing my opinion, especially on Saturday and Sunday, but without effect. The fact is she is worrying over the boys as well as over the war generally and says she starts thinking and then can't rest.

We have heard nothing from Bob for nearly a fortnight and there are constantly rumours of 'heavy firing in the North Sea' where we know he is. Then Wally of course is losing his study as there will be no return to College till after the war is over. In addition he had volunteered for foreign service but Ma doesn't know that and I shall try to keep her ignorant in the hope that he may not have to go. Then Ron is awfully restless and keeps on about Bob and Wally doing something and he nothing for England and though I have reasoned with him quietly about the need of one boy being left to help in case of necessity at home, I shouldn't be surprised to find he had enlisted when he gets back to London. Don't mention the above when you write (about Ron and Wally I mean) or Ma will be worse than ever. . . .

The new law making all Germans register has shown up the number of them there are in England. At Brighton and Hove there were 1200 and this seems to be the case in all big towns. Even at Piltdown there were 2, one supposed to be a lawyer and the other, his brother. . . .

7 September. 8 Powell Road, Clapton, NE.
[Win's home where the Saunders stayed when on visits to London] . . . Last Wednesday Ron tried to get into the London Scottish but it was full. Then he waited in a queue of 500 to try for the Queen's Westminsters from 1 to 4.30, but they were all told to come again tomorrow. On Thursday he went to Great Scotland Yard and joined the

Regulars and was placed in the East Surrey Regiment. His official height was 5' 8½" and chest 35½" and his age was entered as 18.II.29 which was putting it on a few days to make him eligible. . . .

London goes on as usual and the only signs of war are the flags, notices on the taxis and vehicles about enlisting, the recruiting offices and of course the placards carried by the newsboys. Some of the papers deserve suppression for the alarmist headings they put. For instance last night one had a red placard with '15,000 British losses'. Seeing such news thoroughly upsets people with relatives at the front and they naturally thought 15,000 had been lost in a big battle instead of being the total during the campaign.

At Charing Cross the roads were packed for a long distance to see the wounded brought along as a trainload had arrived. Bert, Wally and I went by the London hospital on Saturday and saw a lot of the wounded at the windows in their beds. We were on a bus and could see through the ward.

When you write you might say a good word for Ron to Ma who is very upset about his going. She doesn't understand what a sacrifice it is on his part and doesn't feel proud to have all her sons doing something for their country, even to little Bert who has joined the Scouts for service in Fletching and district. I think she is truly thankful you are safe in Canada so that the fighting blood of the Scotch ancestors can't drive you into 'folly'. I am sending the boys' addresses in case you can write to them. I think Ron needs a letter of encouragement most as he must find it hard to mix with all sorts and conditions. Wally of course is among fellows of his own class and Bob of course is a veteran able to look after himself.

17 September. We returned home on Monday from London and were not sorry to get back to the quiet of the

166

country. You can't live in town at the present time without feeling an atmosphere of restless excitement that tells on the nerves and leaves you tired and more or less irritable and used up. Everywhere you go you see flags flying, appeals to enlist, men in khaki, special constables with their badges, photographs and war telegrams in shop windows and recruiting stations. There are already half a million men enlisted in Kitchener's new army and so great is the rush the authorities are finding a difficulty in dealing with the numbers and are forming camps all over the country.

In this district 6000 troops passed Piltdown on Monday; 2000 artillery with 4000 horses are quartered at Maresfield Park; Lewes is full, troops quartered in every house. One old maid in Lewes who lives in a large house objected on the plea she hadn't had a man in the house for ten years. The unfeeling billeting officer merely remarked 'It's quite time you did' and chalked 8 on the door and 8 very soon arrived.

At Crowborough is another large camp and officers have been to Sheffield Park to spy out the land so we may be a 'garrison town' shortly. At Nutley barbed wire enclosures are being put up to accommodate the flow of German prisoners of war so peaceful Sussex will be a thing of the past before long. . . .

Poor old Ron is finding a soldier's life very hard and in many ways very rough, especially the food and the company as well as much of the language. . . .

11 October. . . . A good story is going the rounds of a Cockney who joined the army and at the end of a week's strenuous marching and drilling and being referred to as No. 254 found himself nodding at his first church parade. Rousing up he heard 'No. 254, art thou weary, art thou languid' and promptly shouted 'not 'arf'. . . .

1 November. . . . Fletching is still very warlike with soldiers passing and repassing. Take this as a sample. Big Room doing an exam, suddenly wild stampede heard in Infant Room, shouts in playground, Master looks out window, sees Governess, Teacher and infants trekking to the gate to cheer a regiment of infantry followed by Red Cross vans. Settled down again then a trampling of horses, a regiment of cavalry; a rest then a rumbling of wheels, a long column of ammunition waggons; later big guns each with 4 horses.

Teacher Kath generally manages to be in the playground when the RFA go by on their horses and it seems to be the usual thing now as they reach the playground coming from Piltdown for every man to 'eyes left' to see if Teacher is looking. One day as I came along there were some field guns outside school with a crowd of children round watching the men eating their dinner. The bell rang for school, the children rushed to join and some of the Tommies pretended to be children and ran too. . . .

We begin to hear many details of the fighting now from the wounded but the majority of them seem to find no words to describe what it is like beyond saying 'it was hell'. As one's experience of hell is limited it is rather difficult to get a picture in your mind. Really the best idea can be formed from the letters picked up on the battlefield from dead Germans, who in their painstaking fashion write down many little things that bring the horrors of war home to you much more clearly than Tommy's stock phrase 'it was hell'. . . .

21 November. . . . The authorities appear to have some information that the Germans mean to attempt a landing and the magistrates have been round to give instructions to special constables of the precautions to be taken and the

plans to be followed should an invasion take place. . . .

4 December. . . . Today it has been blowing a gale and suddenly at 2.30 we had vivid lightning, thunder and sheets of hail and rain. As soon as it abated I sent the children home from school in case of worse weather. Bert, fortunately, was at home today as his bike was under repair. I felt so sorry for him last night. He hadn't got home and as I was feeling uneasy I started to meet him.

He was just coming round the corner carrying his bike which had broken down at Shortbridge. It seems he had been kept in and was coming home alone and the chain broke, then got fixed in the cogs so that he couldn't wheel it. It never struck him to take it in to some house till it could be fetched but he had pluckily tried to drag and carry it the two miles or more. It was blowing hard and he had a long Mac on so by the time he got home he was completely done and just put his head down on the table and sobbed helplessly. After he recovered a bit we sent him to bed and let him remain this morning till he felt ready to move. His bike has been a lot of trouble and I shall be glad when we can get a stronger one for him.

At school we have a money box for the children to put coppers in to buy tobacco for our old boys at the front. This week we sent 3/- to the Weekly Despatch Fund and they send for every 1/6 a Christmas box to any soldier you mention, a Briar pipe, a pouch, 2 oz tobacco, a packet of cigarettes, a packet of matches, so we are hoping two of our boys, Bert Light, 2nd Coldstreams, and Wm Mitchell, 9th Lancers, will have something for Christmas from their old school. The last one to go was Wally Tester. Our old boys' list at present contains the names of 25 in the army and 7 in the navy. . . .

When I was in London I wrote to *The Times* pointing out the unfairness of shutting out short men from the army by fixing the height too high. Others have taken up the point so recently the war office has sanctioned the formation of 'Bantam' regiment of men 5 feet and up. In today's *Times* I see that the 1st battalion was filled up so quickly that a 2nd was opened and again filled up at such a rate that further recruiting has been stopped, at any rate for the present. I think it is a pity short men have been barred so as to have a fine looking regiment of big men. As a short man said to me, 'a big chap takes up as much room in a trench as two my size and we could put in two shots to his one, then to take cover he wants a haystack when a clump of grass would hide us'. . . .

The lists of casualties in *The Times* every day now are very melancholy reading and our losses now number 90,000. As Lord Kitchener thinks the war may last 3 years somebody had pointed out that all our first armies will be gone by that time and the war finished by those raised later. . . .

In 1915 the zeppelin campaign was launched, and between April and October there were intermittent air-raids on the South-East and East Anglia. In two raids on London, on the nights of 7 and 8 September, 38 were killed and 124 wounded. Though puny by comparison with the blitzes of the Second World War, these raids did more than anything to whip up hatred for the Hun. And indirectly they still further widened the gulf between combatants and civilians, who now felt themselves to be in the firing line.

In Goodbye to All That *Robert Graves relates how, on leave in London that September, he found zeppelins and 'business as usual' the main preoccupations. While telling friends of his experiences in the trenches under bombardment, he noticed that, when they realised he was talking about the Western Front, 'the look of interest faded from their faces as though I*

170

had taken them in with a stupid catch.'

With conscription yet to come, any fit young man not in khaki was liable to the ignominy of the 'order of the white feather'. Women increasingly took over jobs normally done by men, and mostly relished their 'emancipation'. It was the beginning of the end for many a pre-war social and moral taboo.

11 January 1915. . . . Well Christmas is over once more and we have had one day at school. I am not sorry it is over as of the many I remember it has been one of the least enjoyable. We closed school on the 23rd. Lu and Nell arrived the same evening, Em and Elsie on the Thursday and Dic on Christmas Day, but no boys for the first Christmas. What a difference it made you can imagine.

We all went to 8.30 celebration instead of the 7. The day passed off very quietly and towards night things began to flag, then 7 Sergeants of the Lancashire Yeomanry called and were invited in and filled the room. Everyone seemed to wake up and the girls especially, even including Elsie who sat on the lap of one named DeCourcy, who comes from Ireland but is of French descent. The girls thoroughly appreciated the military as much as they appreciated what they called a bit of home. None of them had been able to get leave since August so they were rather homesick.

Bert asked one of them what the letters meant on their shoulders, DLOY, and he said Dan Leno's Own Yeoman. He asked another one what MG on his arm stood for and he told him Money Grabber (instead of Machine Gun). Em asked one of them if he found it hard settling down in Sussex and he said he found it harder 'settling up'. One of them had on a new tunic with an upright collar and Nell asked why his collar was different from the others. His companion explained, a man with an upright collar belonged to the staff, had nothing to do and another man was paid to help him do it. They were all fellows in good positions, some in Banks, Post Offices or Mill Owners' sons. Nell told one fellow he didn't seem to have any Lancashire brogue, and he said why should I, I'm Scotch. . . .

Ron arrived home by the 6 train on Thursday but was very unwell, having a severe cold and feverish. Ma kept him in bed most of Friday and it was a bit funny to see his disgust when first thing Ma came in with a bottle of syrup of figs and a dessert spoon. Ron swallowed the first one quietly, gibbed over the 2nd, remonstrated over the 3rd and tried mutiny over the 4th but in they had to go. . . .

18 January. . . . In my last I think I mentioned that Wally Tester had been wounded, since writing I heard the following particulars. His lot were making an attack across open country and as shells were bursting overhead they were ordered to lie down. One of his chums was wounded in the back and called for help so Wally crawled back to him but was wounded in the face by shrapnel which cut his lips, nose and mouth and destroyed the right eye. Mrs Fitzpatrick who happened to be near the French hospital to which he was taken had word from Hilda so visited him and wrote home the particulars. . . .

Today Jimmy Tester came in to show us the letter he had received from Mrs Fitzpatrick. I wish I could send you a copy of the whole letter, the spirit of it was so different from what you would imagine when you remember the 'Miss May' of Sheffield Park. She actually began the letter 'Dear Mr Tester', not as she would have done in former times 'Tester'. Then she went on to describe Wally's injuries and warned them to be prepared to find him disfigured perhaps more than they expected but it would be much in this terrible war to return at all and her husband never would.

Then she went on to enlarge on the pride they would feel

172

that he had played his part as a hero and Wally himself would always be proud of his wounds. She described Wally's pleasure in having a friend from Fletching to visit him and said Wally himself told her he felt much happier wounded and disfigured than he would have done had he stayed at home and done nothing. She promised to visit him again and tried to cheer them up by saying how well he was looked after and what good progress he was making. Altogether it was a good womanlie letter that you felt better for reading. . . .

11 February. . . . Mrs Fitzpatrick is home for a time but is letting her house to some Colonel so I suppose she is going back to France again. She hasn't been able yet to get to the place where her husband is buried and that is her chief object I believe in working in France. . . .

14 February. . . . Wally Tester has been brought to England and is now at Wandsworth but his father and mother have not been up yet as Doctor advised them to wait. The nurse who received him in the French hospital told Mrs Fitzpatrick he was a terrible sight when brought in, so I am afraid his friends will get a shock when they see him, though Doctor says very much is done nowadays in building up parts of the face that have been destroyed. . . .

27 February. . . . On Wednesday Mr Hood and Miss Hilda went to see Wally and the latter came in to tell us about him. She said he was very much shaken and trembled all over as he talked and if anyone spoke to him when he was trying to write, his mind was a blank for a time. He has tubes in the remains of his nose and one in his mouth so that eating and talking are difficult but little can be seen of his face owing to bandages. He was unlucky the other day as in trying to light a cigarette he set his bandages alight

173

and burnt his eyebrows and hair and of course had a nasty shock. . . .

We have been rather excited this week over an air ship which has been passing to and fro all the week. I was just unlocking school on Sunday morning when the children shouted and rushed off down the road so of course I went out to the road to see what was up. The sun was shining brightly and crossing the road to Piltdown apparently at no great height was one of the new air ships, a Parseval I believe. It was made of some shiny metal, aluminium I expect, and was shaped like a fish, and was near enough for us to see the people and the flags. Of course, everyone in the village was soon out and some were speculating if it was a zeppelin.

On Thursday afternoon it passed right over school so low down that we could see the propellers whirling round and the people looking down at the children, who shouted for all they were worth. It seems to have passed to and fro every day but I have not been able to find out why it is patrolling this district. Once can quite understand why zeppelins have not been used so much in the war after watching this vessel, for on Thursday when there was a fairly strong wind on the side of the course it was trying to steer, the effect of the wind on the immense shape was very plainly visible in the way it was carried to the right with a rush every now and again. . . .

We have had several visits from the DLOY especially from Stott and DeCourcy, the former seems to visit Edi more than Ma and myself. . . .

13 March. . . . The camp at Maresfield is now a Canadian Town and the sound of the 'Nasal' will corrupt the pure throaty Sussex in time. With so many horses to feed the district is being scoured for hay and we see their waggons on most days passing to visit the different farms. The first

time they passed school the children cheered and yelled and rather to my astonishment they took absolutely no notice, not one so much as smiling. Our own Tommies always take so much notice and have a lot to say, especially to the teachers.

At Nell's school the RFA from Lewes are full of nonsense when they are off duty and frequently peep through the window. One day a whole company looked in and some of them opened the door, came in and said 'Please Teacher may we come to school'. Of course the children were delighted but Nelly the bashful hid behind a door. Probably your Canadians may be lively when the wet has disappeared for no doubt they have had an experience that is not pleasant. . . .

21 March. . . . Today is simply lovely; nippy first thing, now bright and clear and no wind so that it is difficult to stay indoors at all; you feel you must get all the sun and fresh air possible.

Last Sunday Bert and I went the Mill way for White Violets but only found two or three. Before the end of the week the children at school were bringing Primroses, White Violets and Daffodils and some of the gardens are bright with the pink flowers of the small Dead Nettle. I think the prettiest sight I have noticed this year was a Nut tree hanging over a pond. Of course, it had no leaves but from top to bottom it was draped with very long Catkins swaying in the wind. I wished I could send you a photo of it.

On Sunday morning I was lying in bed with the window open and was very interested watching the Starlings on the tree in the churchyard. There was the coy hen appearing indifferent to the performances of the would-be mates, then the lightning dash of one male at the other followed by the usual flight and pursuit, the return of the conqueror and

175

his swank, the exasperated return of the defeated one and so on. By today the rule of three seems to have worked out and reduced to two birds busily engaged in getting the nest ready.

One evening the air was full of song and I spent some time trying to pick out the different birds but I could only make sure of thrushes one of which was repeating the 'Stick to it' that is so noticeable in some of their songs, the Black-bird whose note seems strangely mournful by the side of the Thrush, the cheery note of the Robin, all the rest a confused jumble of sound with the exasperating 'Jem, Jem' of the Sparrow predominating. This morning I heard the 'Spink, Spink' of the Chaffinch for the first time.

I left this for a few minutes to look at a long line of King Edward's Horse pass by the house, a fine jolly looking lot of men smoking pipes on very fit looking horses and the men laughing and waving to the girls who of course were looking out. No doubt you will think it a good thing they happened along as it switched me off 'Nature'. . . .

31 May. . . . I had headache more or less most of the time in London, then on Thursday a boil or carbuncle made itself felt on the left buttock and has gradually got worse. At school today I couldn't sit down without putting my hands on something and lowering myself gently and getting up in the same performance. I have put a cushion in one of the armchairs and by careful wriggling am managing to write this. . . .

London struck me as very much altered since I was last up. Everywhere you go you meet soldiers in uniform, and it is interesting to look at the badges and try to realise how many different regiments there must be. . . . On St Paul's steps I watched a recruiting meeting for some time. There was a tremendous crowd round and a soldier who looked like a Colonial was letting out for all he was worth. He had a number of men in uniform with him and every little while stopped and pointed his finger at some man in the crowd and shouted 'Why haven't you joined?' Of course everyone looked at the victim who felt called upon to make an excuse if he could, and one of the assistants pushed through the crowd to tackle the one singled out.

One of the funniest things I saw was a big motor transport open truck with some Tommies in, one was playing a mouth organ and four were dancing as though they were in a Ballroom though they were rattling along at full speed. Everyone stopped to laugh but the Tommies took no notice and seemed to be thoroughly enjoying themselves. People were remarking 'Isn't that like them, that's just how they go on at the Front. Aren't they wonderful etc.'. . .

14 June. You will naturally want to have all the news of Ron since he has gone to the front. As far as I can judge he is in or near the small part of Belgium not occupied by the Germans [Ypres]. Of course we are all very anxious as the fighting is now continuous and the losses simply appalling. Every day brings the terrible nature of the war home to us by the people we know who are killed or wounded and by the reports brought home from the front. I write to as many of my old boys as I can so I get a good deal of information that doesn't appear in the papers. . . .

Corporal Mitchell, the second boy of the Piltdown Mitchells, was home from the front last week for three days' leave. He is in the 9th Lancers and was in the famous charge of the Lancers early in the war. He sent me a French and German bullet for the school museum and among other statements said one of the most terrible sights was a shell exploding and arms, legs, heads, flying in the air and sometimes hanging in the trees. . . .

Poor Wally Tester was brought home on Saturday as the doctors can do no more for him in his present condition. He is a physical wreck, thin, bowed, bent, shaky and not pleasant to look at and the worst of it is there are many more worse than he is. . . .

We now have 2,000,000 men in the VTC, which is for men over 40 for Home Defence and the number is every day increasing. Even Fletching has started one and all the places around are doing the same. Our VTC drill on Wednesday evening and Sunday afternoon in the Riding School at Searles, one hour being given to drill and one to shooting. I was sorry to come to the conclusion I was physically unfit owing to my right arm being practically useless at times. . . .

After my last letter you will want to know something of my boils. Well, how Job managed without cursing is beyond me, certainly I didn't and occasionally I couldn't help regretting my stock of swear words were inadequate for what I felt. One thing I learnt about Job that hadn't been plain before was that he didn't have a boil where I did or he couldn't have *sat down*, and he couldn't have listened to his friends' sermons without throwing the Potsheads at their heads. . . .

One thing though amuses me. Doctor ordered me to drink a glass of beer with my dinner. I have always liked to have one but Ma has steadfastly set her face against it as injurious, so it is rather a refreshing experience to find her now insisting on my taking one. Of course I offer a little opposition then 'It's no use what you say, Doctor knows best' and the glass of beer I am quite ready for is plonked down as a sort of forced draught. . . .

26 June. . . . Going to school the other day I met Wally Tester in a bath chair so had to stop to speak to him. I had avoided seeing him up till then as he was very sensitive about meeting people at first. I couldn't describe the alteration, but you can imagine what he is like with one eye gone,

a little piece of his nose near the mouth, then a gap, then a little more nose joining the forehead, his face and hands a bluish grey colour and very emaciated and all energy missing. I did feel for him remembering the smart nice looking fellow he was when I last saw him. . . .

23 July. We have heard pretty regularly from Ron, the last being from the trenches again. He describes the position as a bad one, 200 Germans having been buried near and the smell horrible. They had already had 48 casualties and were burying two more of their men that morning. Bob had written and said he had been a sick boy with a boil on his leg. Wally also had sent and was in good health and spirits. . . .

7 August. . . . The Fletching VTC indulged in extensive cursing on Bank Holiday when they had their first route march. It was raining and they had to march from Searles through the village to Piltdown, on to Newick, out to Chorley, back to Sheffield Park, Sheffield Arms, round Bray's Lane to Searles where refreshments were promised and turned out to be ginger ale and cake. Can you see Mr Fenner, F. Martin, Head, Lainson, Eggleston etc. receiving ginger ale and cake with due gratitude. As Triss reads this I must leave out what they said but perhaps Mr Fenner may tell you when he writes. Mr Fenner prophesies the next route march will consist of the Sergeant Major and Mr Wilson.

20 September. 8 Powell Road, Clapton, NE. . . . Elsie and Art met me at the station. I found very quickly they were both full of the Zep raids of the previous Tuesday and Wednesday and able to talk of little else. Win came along in the afternoon and she was as bad as Em and looked worse as she never had so much colour.

179

As the evening advanced Mr and Mrs Stokes came down to stay till it was time to go to bed which time is between 12 and 1. I got restless and wanted to go outside for a look round but Em made such a fuss I gave up for a time, but a bit later I suborned Stokes and we had a short walk round and found no cause for alarm.

At 12.40 I was supposed to be safe to retire and I was truly thankful as I couldn't see that sitting up and worrying was any help. I thought to myself I will be awake a little while and see if the Search Light is being used, but it was rather a shock to find the sun shining in the window about 6 a.m. and to realise my intended Sentry-go was a failure for I must have dropped off.

However the Zeps had tried but got no nearer than Enfield and I have found that attempts to reach London were made every night of the week. Last week I amused myself by investigating matters, as little or no information can be got from the papers. First I went to Shoreditch High Street, on the route by 35 bus to Liverpool Street. On both sides of the road windows were smashed and a big hole in the road marked the spot where a bus was destroyed. The next point was round Broad Street Station, where the glass in the clock over the Station was wrecked and the buildings much damaged. . . . The worst damage seemed to be an area between Theobalds Road and Holborn where the loss of life must have been serious as it is very thickly peopled. . . .

Usually I persuade Stokes, who is not yet under his wife's control, to take a walk round between 10 and 11, then return and tell them Zeps are turned off for the night, but I can't persuade them to go to bed till after 11, and even then Em doesn't sleep but tortures herself over every sound. One morning at 3 a.m. I heard my door being quietly opened and Em's voice 'Are you all right, Dad?' Em has made up her mind we are not safe at the top of the house if another raid comes but must bolt downstairs just as we are and when she found I meant to dress first said she wouldn't budge till I came down and it would be my fault if she was killed.

What is true of Em, I suppose, is typical of Londoners in general, indeed you hear from conversation in the buses and along the streets the same Nervy ideas. Still everything goes on as usual, same crowds everywhere, places of amusement filled, public's busy, trams and buses going etc. . . .

In November Ron came home on seven days' leave from the front. Inserted here in the typescript copy of the letters is the only one of 'Ma's' letters to William to have survived. In complete contrast to her husband's reflective letter about the same occasion, it is written in staccato style, with dashes taking over from punctuation marks, and gives an instant impression of her energetic, restless, nervous, somewhat domineering personality. In an earlier letter, relating to an August holiday at Eastbourne, Saunders had written: 'If you want to realize Ma and Pa on holiday together, put a Bumble Bee and a Butterfly in a bottle together and watch proceedings.'

30 November. If there is a delay this Mail you must put it down to Ron's arrival home from the Trenches. He came last Thursday night after 23 hrs journey carrying the whole of his Kit, blanket and Macintosh sheet, he looked quite exhausted, however he has just gone again tonight, Tuesday Nov. 30, he goes direct to Win, then to the City tomorrow to do shopping and see Glazebrooke, back to Em for the night and off to France, Thursday midday.

Ron looked splendid today – he has felt well, had 2 changes of clean linen in the few days and slept like a top – the first morning he did not seem to move in bed till 10.30, had breakfast and came down at 12. Friday night Em, Win,

Art, Nell and Lu came and Dic came on Saturday. Em brought a leg of lamb cooked and Dic a chicken and Win fish – we had a very happy time and the only regret was the absent ones – we did not know Ron was coming till we had a wire to send a trap.

The London folks and Dic returned Sunday evening and Nell and Lu Monday morning – after all had gone Ron's things needed cleaning – undergarments were sent out and it needed a carpet brush to get the mud off Mac-rubber, sheet and overcoat. There was gun inspection Saturday evening – Art and Mr Fenner were very keen lookers-on – Elsie made 13 mince pies and sent them over hot on Sunday morning and I had an Xmas pudding saving for Dad's birthday – so we had a sort of Xmas. 8 of us went to early service – Poor Dad knocked up with a bad head – he had not had one since the summer holiday – there was great excitement and late hours and on Saturday Dad, Ron, Art and Nell went to Uckfield to get hair cut – and Ron wanted to do the generous and got a Motor Car to bring them back.

Ron seemed to quite recuperate yesterday and was singing about the house to the top of his voice which reminded me more of you Will than Wally – he seemed to love wandering about the attics and exploring the apple cupboard, he said it reminded him of lots of things he, Bob and Wally used to do in those attics – he seems to have seen enough of the battlefield and Trench life – he has 9 or-derlies under him and works between times in the Trench Orderly room which is a dug out.

He says he shall send in an application at the first oppor-tunity and try to get to General Headquarters on the Clerical staff entirely – and I certainly hope he does – one day they caught rain water in his Mac-sheet and then made tea of it – we did hear some yarns probably Dad can remember them better when he writes you – he had some narrow escapes – and then another minute – he would say that one fellow who always said his prayers was quickly killed – he was full of funny tales and a rare mixture.

Mother

12 December. Your last letter spoke of the Photos of Ma and myself and Bob. . . . We did not ask Ron to have one taken when he was at home it is much nicer to picture him as he was in his last Photo before he had gone through the terrible experiences all our men at the front have to bear. Whatever Newspaper writers may say you may take my word for it no one can ever look the same again after seeing the awful slaughter of a modern battlefield, hearing the noise of 1000 guns firing high explosives, and living in the Trenches.

I sat and watched Ron when he first came home and tried to note the change in him, and I also closely watched him all the time so as to form a very clear idea of him to tell you when I wrote. It made me feel awfully sad to note many things none of the others would notice in their delight in seeing him. He used to sit hunched up towards the fire, every now and then holding his hands to the blaze, his face seemed unnaturally long, nose prominent, black marks under his eyes, hair rough and badly cut, and quite content just to sit and talk.

All he seemed to want was to be at home and rest, and though perhaps he may not own it to you, he doesn't want to go in the Trenches again and would gladly return to civil life again. We did all we could to strengthen him up but the time was all too short, and though he tried not to show it, he felt parting keenly. He has a most extraordinary love of home and has apparently always been like it, though among so many we haven't noticed it, and in thinking things over, I am wondering sometimes if it isn't kinder to children to try to make home less the 'Home Sweet Home' of the poet.

A little point about Ron before he went struck me as

183

typical, he went up to the Attic and stayed some time, and I found he was trying to reconstruct some of the scenes he had played there with Bob and Wally. He let this out unconsciously, and I know he was always trying to form a mental picture of home to carry back with him. . . .

By 1916 conscription and an intensification of State control, which now regulated almost every facet of civilian life, were accepted as harsh necessities as victory seemed more than ever elusive in the stalemate of trench warfare.

Though the great Somme offensive brought bereavement on a vast scale to homes throughout the country, the sporadic zeppelin raids remained an obsessive talking-point (they figure largely in Saunders' letters during the year). Prices continued to rise, austerity became a patriotic duty, but there was as yet no food shortage and no rationing.

Conscription left a diversity of manpower gaps to be filled by women. In February there was a call for 400,000 women for agricultural work, and the phenomenon of the 'land girl', actually wearing trousers, became an accepted part of the country scene.

23 January. I wish you could have been with me this afternoon for the walk to Piltdown and round Daleham. Little birds were singing and an occasional thrush was trying to get his voice in order, and there was plenty of activity among other birds deficient in song. Going down Rushing Brook my eye was caught by something unusual on top of the tall furze, so motioning Bert to be quiet we got close and made out a large squirrel-coloured mouse with a long furry tail busily employed feeding on the furze blossoms. He or she did not see us so we watched it a long time but we didn't recognise the kind and one of the schoolboys who

happened to pass said he had never seen one like it. . . .

3 February. I daresay you often wonder how life goes on with us here at home and whether we feel the war in any special way. Well, there is not the feverish rush for papers as formerly owing to the absence of important news. The censorship is so strict that much of the interest in the reading of War News has been destroyed.

English people taken as a whole are only just beginning to realise the magnitude of the struggle we are engaged in, and of course want to blame somebody else that greater things are not being done to end the War. This week the papers are full of the Zep attacks on the Midlands, and there is a general feeling of exasperation at our failure to prevent the raids. In the Mail today there are a number of letters calling for reprisals as the only way of protecting our women and children, and though the Government has so far refused to follow German frightfulness, public opinion will eventually compel them to return raid for raid. . . .

Bert and I walked up the village and round Daleham on Sunday and met the Fletching Home Defence marching with Rifles to Piltdown where they joined up with the Uckfield force for manoeuvres behind the Chapel. I met Bob Burley who gave it as his opinion, 'If England has to fall back on they chaps, we be done'. . . .

24 February. . . . I was talking to a cousin of your friend Hudson, and he had just come from Norfolk where the Zep raid was. She said 14 bombs dropped in a field near their house, and the field was torn into great chasms. The farmer had been burning heaps of rubbish so the Zeps evidently thought they were destroying a town.

John Bull last week had an article by a Clergyman urging the duty to attack the Germans in every way possible, and

185

in the course of it he spoke as follows:

'Damn everything, except the task of damning and blasting for all time the arch devil of Potsdam, the gang of murderers who surround him, and the legions of ferocious, pitiless rapers, burners, torturers and baby stabbers who obey his Imperial Hell's inspired will.'

Such language of course is altogether unusual in an English paper but I have quoted it to show the blind passionate fury that the majority of people who pass through a Zep raid feel towards the Germans. . . .

3 March. . . . As you say my taste in Pipes has altered, but the change has been mainly brought about by stern necessity. As the teeth wear out it behoves the wise smoker to hunt for a pipe that shall impose no undue strain on the remaining teeth, hence my quest in London for a light perfectly balanced pipe with a fairly wide mouthpiece. I have smoked my two pipes regularly since Christmas and am still satisfied with them. . . .

21 March. . . . I don't know of a single article that has not gone up in price, so that it is a case of 'needs must' with the many people over Economy. On the other hand many of the working classes were never so well off as they are now, but these are not the country farm hands but the people near the Munition Works where boys and girls of fourteen are earning 30/- to 40/- a week and men earn up to £5 or £6. Labour is coming into its own, there is no doubt, but what is going to happen after the war, when wages once more fall to the old levels? If the worker is wise enough to save there ought to be a big Empire planting movement, the possession of means enabling those whose occupation of Munition making is gone to start in one of our Colonies a more useful life. . . .

28 March. . . . This last page is written specially for Triss in the hope it will save her from misunderstanding the Saunders Character of which I expect you have a share though fortunately for you there is a possible mixture of the Francis strain that may save you from falling into disgrace with your wife as I have done.

From both my Father and Mother I inherited a very strong dislike to show how deeply I felt anything, we were brought up to bear pain without showing it, and learnt to dread showing our feelings as a sign of weakness. The consequence has been that all my life the more I feel the less I seem able to express my feelings. I daresay you are wondering what all this is leading up to, so I won't waste more time and go straight ahead.

Ma's birthday is with her a very great matter, and for days before she is thinking of it, and counting up the letters and presents she will receive. It came on Thursday, and happened in the week I had been poulticed for 3 days for an abscess on the lower jaw. I had eaten no solid food and got into such a perspiration that I never properly undressed, having got into bed in my flannels.

On Wednesday night I had stripped for the first time and put on a Night Shirt and was hoping for a night's rest. However Ma had Birthday on the brain, and couldn't sleep, first she thought the spirit lamp was open and must be shut up, then she suddenly sprang up at 1 a.m. saying the room was too close and slung the window open with a bang.

Just after 5 a.m. she started making tea, and while I was in a half dazed state I heard a very peremptory voice say 'Here, drink this.' I struggled up and found a saucer of hot fluid poked in my hand which I obediently swallowed and its nauseous character woke me up completely. A minute after the same voice said 'Here's your tea' and gladly I swallowed it to wash out the remembrance of the other stuff.

Then I found I had swallowed a strong dose of Kruschen

Salts, which as perhaps you know are composed of 7 different ingredients, any and all of which are capable of exercising the power of the Hyssop mentioned by the Psalmist. I never have been able to take Salts and their effect on me was instantaneous. What was left of me got back to bed shivering with cold, and holding both arms round what was once a stomach.

Now comes the point – The wife of my bosom, who opens her birthday by pouring seven devils into a trusting husband's stomach, complains 'You have not wished me many happy returns of the day.' Could I wish for such returns with the 7 still going for all they were worth in my suffering interior? I couldn't, but there was not enough of me to argue the point, so I held on like grim death to my hip bones, to save the walls of the stomach from being rent. I took all the Lecture on my want of feeling in silence, no back answers, but saved it all up, till my stomach was able to look after itself.

It is painful to me to write of such matters but I want to save you from similar affairs, and the Moral for Triss is, 'Salts and Sentiment won't work together.'

28 April. Clapton, London. Ma's letters will have told you I have had all my teeth extracted and have been away from home for a fortnight. . . .

All this week the weather has been lovely, and as the Barometer has risen it is what is known as zep conditions. We had our first experience on Tuesday. . . . At 11.15 I was roused by heavy firing, so got up and lighted a candle. Then I roused Bert and started him dressing and began to put my own things on. Then we heard Art and the others rushing downstairs, then Em calling upstairs for us to hurry, to put out the light, not to stop to dress, etc., all in a high-pitched voice of excitement.

I got all my clothes on except collar, then went down into

188

the basement where I found them all just as they jumped out of bed. All the time the guns were roaring and poor Bert was quite ill with fright. In about a quarter of an hour the firing stopped, so I went out on the steps to look round, but there was nothing to be seen, or heard. . . .

As regards myself, I did not feel so alarmed as I expected, and did not experience the 'Nerves' afterwards they all seem to suffer with. While I am writing we can hear guns firing but whether for practice or otherwise no one knows.

4 June. Nell and Ma no doubt send you full accounts of Bob's visits. Everyone seems to admire him, that is, his appearance and people turn round to have a second look. He stands 6 feet in spite of the usual sailor's round shoulders, and has really a fine open countenance, which in repose has the intent look of one who has watched, and known danger. At times he has all the nonsense of the boy you know, at others he is the sailor full of his work and wanting to talk of nothing else.

When we were walking out to Piltdown he was very quiet and when I looked at him he said 'Seems I just would like to drop in and see "Old Will" and Triss, Dad.' I expect the walk reminded him of the many walks you had had when he used to tread on your stick etc. . . .

We begin to see the effect of the Groups being called up even in Fletching, first one well-known face and then another disappearing. Mr Fenner has been very emphatic over employing 'Lady' helpers on his farm, no he wouldn't etc., now his better half says he has engaged one. You would smile to see them, they wear thick boots, leggings, knee breeches (corduroy), a short smock, and a soft hat. There is a farm at Danehill training them. The one I saw would have passed for a man anywhere.

16 July. . . . The War is every day pressing harder on

189

everyone in so many ways which it is needless to specify beyond the fact that since the big offensive started we hear the guns all day sometimes, and can't forget that Ron is there. And we are dreading the Telegram that so many have received lately. We had a long letter from him this morning, a copy of which you shall have and though it is a great relief to know he has got through so far, yet there is the knowledge that the same dangers have to be gone through again and again. . . .

On Saturday I went to London and saw the Dentist who said the Gums had shrunk so much I must have a fresh impression. . . .

In the afternoon London Bridge Station was just plug full and I spent about 40 minutes going about in the crowd. There were soldiers of all kinds going and coming with Canadians, Australians, etc., Red Cross men and Military Police, people coming to meet some, others seeing friends off. Only one thing struck me as comical and that was a Scotchman who rolled out of the refreshment room with a waiter to help him. He reminded me of a big edition of Harry Lauder and looked as though dressed for the stage, which in his case had evidently been the Trenches.

He was fairly big, nose especially, had an enormous Tam o' Shanter over most of his face, very thick hairy bare legs, and the kilt of a man many sizes smaller than himself. The waiter propped him against the wall and left him to an English chum, who was not so far gone as Sandy. He pitched Sandy's Tartan round him, then admired his struggles to pick up his ticket which he had dropped. When that was safely accomplished there were the heavy kit bags and coats to negotiate, but as Sandy after his struggles with the ticket seemed past further exertions, the chum who was immensely powerful threw the coats over his shoulder, got one kit bag in his arms and threw the other on his shoulder.

Then came the most comical sight of all. Sandy, carrying

190

nothing, followed by his laden chum, charging right through the crowd to the train, smiling and talking to everyone with much condescension and complacency. You could not help feeling sorry to see such brave fellows in such a condition, but at the same time it was irresistibly comical. . . .

3 August. . . . We hear the guns of the great offensive most days and to me it often sounds like the thud of some giant propeller, but it is curious how the intensity of the sound varies in different parts of the village. . . .

Ron's last letter came today, and he said he was expecting to go in the Trenches the day after he wrote, and that a 15 inch gun was firing on one side and a 12 inch on the other. . . .

13 September. . . . Our Casualty Lists are very, very heavy every day and we continually hear of those we know being killed. Two of my old boys have just been killed, Gray and Tadgem (both lived near the Station). Robin Kenward is still missing and Ron thinks he must have been killed. We heard from Ron last week, quite a long cheerful letter and saying he was enjoying the parcel we sent off in Eastbourne. . . .

I expect you will begin to wonder why I haven't mentioned Ma yet. All last week she was full of things that must be done (the girls had Spring Cleaned throughout while we were away) but arguing with a wife with House mania is useless. Accordingly she would begin to move several hours before it was necessary in holiday time and though I tried once or twice to pretend to be asleep, it was no good, as she would sit on the side of the bed and massage her foot and leg with Elliman's, causing the bed to go up and down, and my liver and temper too.

Bert was called to light the fire and I intended to get the

breakfast when he had got a start. The first morning I didn't start soon enough for her ladyship, who started dressing at 'Catch the train' speed. She got her blouse half on, then started downstairs getting her other arm in as she went and calling out to me there was plenty of room for me to dress. I accordingly did but. . . .

27 September. Clapton, London. . . . At midnight we went out again to the corner of the High Road and got back to the house when we heard some people across the way saying excitedly, Yes it is, No, Yes, look, so we went over to see what they were looking at. Just then the Search Light shot out and guns began to bang, so we skipped indoors in a hurry and found them all huddled in the passage in dread. I couldn't see any sense huddling there and dreading Bombs that weren't near perhaps, so I slipped upstairs to the top back window where I could see the Orient Search Light.

I found it directed a little to the right of that Steeple in the High Rd and following the beam saw it had spotted a Zep which looked like a silver cloud. . . .

Now as to how one feels in a Raid, as far as I was concerned, I was not frightened or nervy but excited. To some people it is evidently otherwise, their judgement seems to go, and you can't reason with them. If you say the explosions are a long way off and the Search Lights are pointing miles away all they say is, There might be other Zeps right overhead etc. Shakespeare was right when he said 'Cowards die many deaths.'

It is, I suppose a matter of temperament and I am thankful mine allows me to keep cool and not worry about what might happen. Don't you think I am trying to boast of being braver than other people, but I had been curious to know how I should feel in a raid, so now I know. You will get full accounts in Sunday's paper but in the 2 raids 74

192

were killed and 152 injured.

18 November. . . . I would like you to be present when we have some of the wounded soldiers to tea. . . . We are sitting round a big fire of logs after tea. Billy the Canadian has been talking of every subject under the sun, while Mac, the North Countryman has been silent. Suddenly he feels he ought to take part in the conversation which he does forthwith as follows (but which I can't write as he said it). 'I was kept in bed till I got tired of it so I waited till the Matron was out then I got one of the chaps to put me in a Bath Chair and run me round the grounds. I was enjoying myself when suddenly he sees the Matron coming, so the first thing I know he shoves me behind a bush and says "Stay there you booger" . . . '.

Ma says Ssh . . . , the girls giggle, Billy looks ready to burst with laughter, Mac suddenly conscious he has said a swear word, looks horribly uncomfortable and dries up, while Pa tries to relieve the tension by talking quickly about something else. . . .

Just at present it is like old times at Fletching. A Play or Operetta is being got up for Christmas and all our lot are in it. Edi is the Hero of the piece, Prince Shee-ma-quin, and as she couldn't pronounce it properly I told her to say She-may-grin, which she is quite likely to do. Bert is the Lord High Executioner, while Lu and Kath are maids of honour to the Princess.

We have been expecting Bob all day but he hasn't come yet. Wally's last mail went down in the *Arabia* so we haven't heard for a fortnight. Ron is in the Trenches again. Shall we ever see you all home together? I do miss the Boys.

Kiss all the Bairns for Grandpa.

Throughout 1917 the war of attrition on the Western Front, cul-minating in the horrific Third Battle of Ypres, July to Novem-

ber, drained away much of what remained of the fit male population. A contemporary writer described Britain as 'a country of women, old men, boys and children, with a sprinkling of men in khaki.'

To the legions of women in men's jobs (from munitions workers to land girls, policewomen to bus conductresses) were now added the women's uniformed services. Largest of these was the Women's Auxiliary Army Corps (WAAC).

The launching of Germany's campaign of unrestricted warfare on shipping by U-boats, in answer to the Allied blockade, made food shortages and soaring prices generally a major preoccupation. 'Eat Less Bread and Victory is Secure' was a typical poster.

To the zeppelin threat were now added fleets of German bombers. There were four heavy raids on London in September, where thousands now took shelter in the Underground at night.

11 January. . . . Bob had come down in a Special from Scotland with 700 Jack Tars and his arrival took everyone by surprise as only the day before he had said in a letter he couldn't tell when his leave started. Ma and the girls thought he was looking thin and ill when he arrived. To my eye he looked as well as could be expected considering the strain he has to bear in the North Sea.

His ship is one of the First Battle Squadron, carrying 15 inch guns and Torpedoes and they are always prepared to meet the German Fleet which always tries to evade them, their aim being to catch part of our Fleet inferior to them. Bob tells very little but Harry Stevenson and his chum were in to tea on Monday and were talking together of going into action a short time back. All acknowledge they felt nervy, Harry was in a Turret, Bob in the Conning Tower, and George up aloft. Just as they were getting into range, a Zeppelin spotted them so the Germans scuttled off, leaving their Submarines to try their luck, but though one was seen on each side they were not hit.

The only difference I noted in Bob was a deep furrow across his forehead but otherwise he was the same old 'Grin' with the same love of fooling as ever. The girls chaffed him about being fond of the girls, and there may be some reason in their chaff as his arm seems to slip naturally round Elsie Fenner's waist when she sits near him. . . .

My last picture of Bob is when I came down just after 7, he is sitting on a chair by the fire staring at vacancy and very miserable. At breakfast he eats less than usual, and holds Lu's hand, or puts his arm round Edi, and when the latter says something funny, he laughs hysterically and takes the opportunity to wipe his eyes with a handkerchief. The trap arrives, he hurriedly kisses us, and blunders into the trap. In spite of his bigness he is just as homesick as ever, and I am afraid we feel the parting just as much. He was awfully disappointed Ron hadn't come, but you can imagine our delight when a wire came this evening, Ron just arrived at Em's. . . .

27 January. Ron must be the subject, I suppose, to begin with, but as doubtless Ma and the girls have already written you about his visit I must try to picture him rather than the visit.

He is altogether much older, has very strong opinions, is very determined and, it must be confessed, somewhat 'high and haughty' as becomes a British NCO, talks incessantly, smokes ditto, drinks beer, wine, spirits, like his father, is perfectly self-possessed, enjoys a good meal, a good fire, and a spoon with a nice girl. The thing that I think would strike you most is the freedom from shyness in showing his affection. Next to myself I think he was always what Ma calls the Coldest of all our family, but perhaps Triss has discovered 'Still waters run deep.' When Ron arrived he

195

put his arms right round me and hugged me and did the same when he left.

During his stay he was always hugging and kissing Ma and the girls. His greatest happiness was when we all sat round the fire and talked, especially of ancient family history when they were boys and the mischief they got into. On the Sunday when Dic and Elsie were here we sat round a blazing fire, Elsie's head on one shoulder and Dic's on the other and Ron's arms round them. . . .

Thanks very much for what you suggest about my teeth, but I am very glad to say I am getting more comfortable and find that a file and some Emery paper are more effective than a visit to the Dentist. . . .

4 March. . . . We heard from Wally today. He was very well and was expecting to start on a Trek doing so many miles a day under war conditions. From Ron we only get PCs so expect he is in the Trenches. He is in the sector where all the advance has been made lately. . . .

11 March. . . . You would have enjoyed seeing Ma's face one morning last week. She had kept worrying because Dic hadn't written. When the post came there was a PC from Dic. Ma was sitting up in bed while I was dressing, so I took the PC and read out, 'Sorry I haven't written but Harold and I got quietly married yesterday.' Ma took it in, but had a lot to say when she got hold of the card and read it for herself. . . .

9 April. . . . Now I am going to describe for Triss how I was punished for trying to deceive my wife. I have often told you Ma has a habit of getting up early and hustling everybody directly holidays begin. I did so want a good rest last night that I was wicked enough to put the clock an hour slow and went to bed gloating over the extra rest I should

get. Being overtired of course I couldn't get to sleep for some time, then dozed on and off till 2 a.m. when I found myself wide awake with my arm and legs aching. I kept as still as possible but found Ma was awake, too, and we neither of us went to sleep again the rest of the night, so my plan failed miserably. . . .

13 May. . . . I pictured Triss and the children out with me this afternoon across the fields stopping every few yards to pick some of the following, Daffodils, Primroses, Cowslips, Ramshorns, Anemones, Bluebells, Vetches, Celandines, Heartsease, Stitchwort, Marsh Marigolds, Ladies Smocks, etc., and of course Daisies. The Dandelions are in grand form and make some of the fields a blaze of yellow. In all my years of country life I can safely say I never saw such a profusion nor so many varieties in bloom at once.

The views over the Park are a never ending pleasure to me as I smoke my pipe in the garden. The trees are just breaking into leaf and with the bright sunshine there are all shades of green and apparently pale yellow relieved here and there with the sombre hue of a solitary pine, or the white looking leaves of the Poplar. If I turn round and look across the gardens there are the snowy blooms of Pear, Plum and Cherry contrasted with the pink buds of the Apple. It all seems so specially wonderful this year, probably because of our trying winter when deadness and dullness were the prevailing impressions. . . .

20 May. . . . On Wednesday morning while I was dressing I was looking out of the window as the Postman came along. I saw him give Grover the Butcher some letters and among them an Official Envelope. This he put down thinking it was from the War Office about sheep and cattle as he had had several. They let it lie till dinner time then opened it and found it was a notice to say Harry, the

youngest boy, was killed in France on the 8th. Poor old Grover was so upset and can't seem to get over it, if anyone tries to sympathise he stands and cries. . . .

27 May. . . . Housekeeping is a trial, not only increased prices but some articles not obtainable. One week no butter or margarine. Last week I could get no BDV tobacco here and Bert tried two shops at Uckfield but failed. Sugar and treacle are always difficult to get, so I have at last given up sugar in tea. Meat is very dear so we are gradually becoming temperate in many ways. I still drink Stout but a bottle has to last three times as long. I wish sometimes I could like water and drop Beer entirely, but Ma thinks I ought to keep to Beer as I don't eat a big meal at any time. . . .

10 June. Last week I spoke of the gunfire in France and the papers have already told you of the great attack at Messines. Yesterday and today we have been free from it and you can hardly imagine the relief it has been to me. The continued pulsation, like the sound of a great propeller on a mammoth Steamer, seemed never to stop night or day, and though, strange to say, many people didn't seem affected, others were as sensitive as I was. But one thing of course is what a weight has been taken off our minds now that Ron is in England for a special course of field training and will be for some months, we hope. I posted a *Daily Mail* to you on Thursday and marked what should please you, viz. Ron mentioned in Despatches. . . .

8 July. . . . We had a short scribble from Win to say they were safe but had been terrible scared, the fleet of Aeroplanes passing over them and the noise was terrible. . . . I am afraid the Government has been making a mistake over the temper of the people in not returning Raid for Raid,

and there will be riots and wild scenes to bring them to their senses. . . .

23 July. . . . Today 12 Aeroplanes passed over in a body going towards London so we are wondering if there is anything on. The Bombardment has been very heavy again all day and at times is most worrying to the ears and head. When it started on Monday evening little Elsie was out with Bert up the hill above the Mill but was so frightened she bolted straight home arriving nearly exhausted and streaming with perspiration. She thought there was a big Air Raid and I had to convince her it was nothing of the sort. To hear it you can hardly realise that the firing is in France or Belgium.

One of the mothers brought me her boy's photo and apologised because he didn't call on me when he was home from the front where he had been 2 years before getting leave. He is in the 16th Lancers and she said she nearly cried to see the change in him, all the Boy being gone. He couldn't bear to come down the Street to see anyone and was very downhearted to go back. She said the sound of the Guns all day long when she was alone nearly drove her mad thinking of her boy out there. . . .

29 July. . . . The Gunfire on the Belgium coast some days is very terrible, especially from 7 till 9 p.m., and often with it are long explosions and occasionally the sound of what appears a mammoth gun. . . .

12 August. . . . Bob is home on leave and wanted to go to Brighton for the day. We rested on the beach for some time but there are too many of all sorts and conditions there for one to enjoy the rest. Owing to the Raids all the South Coast places are crowded, and of course the Munitioners are nowadays millionaires and can afford to spend freely.

But notices were up 'No one is allowed to spend more than 1/3 on food.' With the cost of living you can figure out the quantity supplied. . . .

While I was talking to Mitchell one morning a woman came along and asked to speak to me. She complained the boys had been calling after her, and every time she went up the Street they shouted 'Tart'. I had a bother to keep from smiling, as that is the general name for her in the village. Her husband is the coalman and she is one of those dirty untidy kind of women who dress up occasionally and make eyes at the soldiers.

I advised her to get her husband to clout them well, but she said they didn't do it when he was with her, but I said, never mind, tell them their names and he can drop on them when he meets them. Of course I talked to them when I got to school, but legally I have no power over them out of school hours. . . .

19 August. . . . Last Thursday a gentleman at Piltdown invited 'Arms and Legs', i.e. soldiers who had lost an arm or a leg, to play a Cricket Match in the Recreation Ground. They came up in a big Motor Charabanc from Brighton. There was a big crowd to see them and the schoolchildren, at Lu's instigation, brought plums, apples and pears which they distributed ad lib.

I stood and watched for a time but it was too worrying to me to see a man on one leg trying to bat, though Jim Fuller our captain told the bowlers to bowl easy balls. Some of the women cried to see them but they were as cheerful as crickets and hopped on one leg from the Pavilion without crutches.

You know how our ground is situated, a lovely view of the Downs, ladies in white sitting round the ground, and the wounded who were not playing scattered here and there receiving plenty of sympathy from all the girls. All the time the big guns were roaring in Flanders so we could hear the War and see the sad results of it.

To show the way the wounded look at things: Nell remarked to one about the way he manicured his nails. His chum remarked directly, 'It's nothing to the way I keep mine' and held up his hand with all the tops of the fingers gone. . . .

23 September. . . . During the week there have been several reminders winter is coming. The Robins have come round again making their little mournful songs, and one kept me company in the garden. The swallows are collecting round the Church Spire and evidently practising for the long journey that is to come. The Caterpillars are beginning to disappear, and a stray wasp now and then blunders into the house. Just lately the Cadets seem to have adopted Fletching as the place to spend a week end, or to have a little jollification, so the Griffin is flourishing and the girls are happy. . . .

The guns are going again as I write so I am afraid there is another raid in progress somewhere. Thousands of people have left London till the end of the Harvest Moon so as to be out of the danger zone. Brighton is simply packed with Jews from the East End. By the end of last week there was actually a dearth of food, some of the shops having no tea, sugar or provisions and the Butchers were asking and getting exorbitant prices for meat. . . . I never remember people hating the coming of winter so much as they do this year. . . .

15 October. . . . Lu leaves next Friday to join up in the WAAC as a Clerk but Ma will tell you all about that. . . .

22 October. . . . Lu left on Friday and Ma wept after she had gone. Personally I had tried to dissuade Lu from

joining up, but seeing she was determined gave up. . . .

Last Tuesday one of Lu's 'Boys' came to see us straight from the Trenches. He had had 5 weeks in the front line and told me they were firing for 2 hours right off with their 12 Machine Guns. Every gun fires 600 shots per minute so you can imagine what the ground in front of them was like after 6 counter-attacks by the Germans had been attempted. . . .

16 November. . . . We are very much cast down, Mr Hood dying yesterday. You can understand how we all feel his loss as he was so unlike any of the clergy we have been connected with and he was so interested in all our family. He has never been the same since his youngest son was killed and when Lu went to say Goodbye he gave her the impression he had no wish to live and expected the end soon. His death has broken one more link with Fletching and I shall not be sorry when the time comes for me to leave it. . . .

25 November. . . . Lu writes very cheerfully from France. Both her admirers had written *serious* letters to her and a Scotchman who sat next to her in the office waxed sentimental occasionally. . . .

28 December. As far as weather was concerned we had an old-fashioned Christmas, bitterly cold with snow and frost about. Ron came along unexpectedly on Christmas Eve. . . . He was never of a very humble disposition and now he is an officer I am afraid he will be what his sisters call 'Some Swank'. He has very decided views on most things and a very decided way of expressing them. . . .

In spite of the War there was the usual present-giving and everyone seemed to enjoy it. I had suggested it should be dropped this year but the whole force of family scorn was directed on me, with Ma leading the attack, so I had to subside feeling somewhat of an old Scrooge. Even Bert, though 15, quite looked forward to having his stocking hung up and thoroughly enjoyed going through it on Christmas morning. 12 of us sat down to Turkey dinner etc., and a sort of shadow of a Plum Pudding. . . .

Later Mrs Fenner, Mrs Saunders, Daisy and Mrs Cowtan called. They are all very down on me about going to London because of the Air Raids, but, with all respect to Triss, it is not good for man to live with 7 or 8 ladies for too long a period. I am bound to get away for a few days if I am to keep sane, and it would take more than Air Raids to stop me. . . .

In mid-April 1918, with the Allied armies reeling back before the Germans' all-out offensive, the war reached its lowest ebb with Haig's chilling orders to his troops: 'With our backs to the wall and believing in the justice of our cause, each one of us must fight to the end.'

On the Home Front, too, backs were to the wall. Near-starvation loomed, and it was only the introduction of rationing that saved Britain from the sufferings of the German civilian population. By July only bread, cheese and tea remained un-rationed. A severe shortage of coal (already rationed) was an additional privation.

Conscription was extended to men up to fifty-one years old. How far the country now depended on its womenfolk was demonstrated in June, when a 3000-strong procession, repre-senting all branches of women's war work, paraded in London. It was noted that there was not a petticoat to be seen.

As the war drew to a close a disaster struck that no one could have foreseen: 'Spanish Influenza'. Within a few months the disease, for which there was no known remedy, had killed over seventy million world-wide. In Britain the air-raids, over which there had been such hysterical reactions, could now be seen as of fractional import. By May 1919, when the epidemic abated, the British death-toll had reached nearly 200,000. On the fighting fronts, during the four years, three months and seven days of the war, the British dead had numbered 744,000.

The war weariness that had overtaken the Home Front by 1918 is dramatically reflected in Saunders' letters. Much of their sparkle has gone. They are briefer, more disjointed, with few anecdotes, and suggest a gritting of the teeth not only in anticipation of the ending of the war but of his planned retirement by Christmas.

The letters are largely concerned with family affairs (even the arrival of the Americans, who were to tip the scales of victory on the Western Front, rate only a passing mention). Bert has left school and home to work in a bank in Lewes. Ron has obtained his wings in the RAF, and is patrolling the Channel in an airship. Bob has transferred from the battleship Royal Sovereign to a destroyer, in which he complains of sea-sickness. Wally, after four uneventful years in India, is ending his war uneventfully in Mesopotamia. Lu writes infrequently from France.

Vegetable growing (now a grim necessity) has largely taken over from nature rambles, and even these are described in a lack-lustre way. On the marital front a kind of stalemate seems to have been reached, with only two episodes worthy of note.

The only letter that stands out is that relating to Armistice Day, 11 November, which reads like a long sigh of relief. A few extracts will suffice to lead up to that long-awaited culmination.

5 January. Clapton. . . . Before Win's New Year's party Will was sent out to get a bottle of wine or some spirits and after a long time came back with a bottle of Gingerette which was all he could get. The evening was spent in singing before and after supper and at 12 we went outside

to listen for any sound to usher in the New Year but fear of
Air Raids kept everything still. There was general hand-
shaking and kissing, Auld Lang Syne, and, last, toasting
the New Year in Gingerette, with apologies from Will that
it wasn't something stronger. . . .

26 January. We have had a whole week of mild weather. It
is a luxury again to have your bedroom window wide open
all night especially when you remember a few days ago the
window was shut and a big fire burning night and day. Ma
started one when I was in London and kept it up till last
Saturday, besides wearing underclothes, night dress,
dressing jacket and shawl in bed, while poor Pa just had a
night shirt, generally unbuttoned. I hate a fire burning at
night, the flame flickering seems to make my eyes ache and
I can't really rest properly, but men with cold wives have to
submit. It has been a most tiring week and I am very
thankful to get it over. . . .

30 March. . . . I saw in the Sussex papers the Cuckoo was
heard at Cross-in-Hand a few days ago, but probably it was
a bird that wore trousers as many Sussex boys are fond of
imitating the Cuckoo. So far I have seen one Blackbird's
egg, but it is a puzzle for the birds to find a hedge with suf-
ficient cover to build their nests nowadays. . . .

1 June. . . . The Cuckoos are in great force this year and
everybody agrees they never saw or heard so many. The
great blot on everything is the thud and throb of the guns,
night and day, in France and yesterday I could even hear
them indoors. Aeroplanes are constantly going over and
will soon be as common as Motors and attract as little attention. . . .

7 September. . . . There was never a time in England when

vegetables were so plentiful owing to all vacant land being used as allotments till the end of the war, and yet I never saw such high prices for the commonest vegetables. In spite of our boasted Food Control there is undoubtedly a lot of profiteering. Ma paid 7d for one apple one day. . . .

19 October. . . . Ma has had a bustle on most of the week, so we slower people have to take cover when we can. I had a narrow escape last night of being brought in guilty of want of sympathy etc. Ma had a big saucepan of boiling water on and a bowl of onions ready to put in the saucepan. She stood the onions down, hustled around for a shovel of coke, took the lid off the saucepan, and shot in the coke. . . .

27 October. . . . The Influenza Plague is rampant in Sussex, nearly all the schools round are closed and there is hardly a house that isn't affected. In Fletching Harry Scutt and old Reed have died. Head, the cowman at Mr Fenner's, suddenly fell dead while at work. . . .

9 November. . . . There was great excitement on Thursday when a rumour was circulated that Peace had come. When the news reached Maresfield Camp the cheering could be heard at Piltdown. Then on Friday everyone was disappointed to find the news was untrue. . . .

16 November. I expect you are wondering how we all feel over the Armistice. The news reached Fletching about 11.40 a.m., and was soon brought down to School where the Union Jack was at once hoisted and the children cheered loud enough to be heard all over the parish.

When I came home to dinner everyone was out putting up flags and colours, and though people were excited, there was no noise till a scratch team started to ring the Bells. I had doubts about my right arm and hand so didn't help but tried to get my dinner quietly but Ma and the girls couldn't sit still and kept rushing to the door to see what was going on.

The children were not very keen on Lessons in the afternoon so I gave an address on the War and the Armistice after which we sang Patriotic Songs. Then we all adjourned to the Church to take part in an interesting ceremony.

On the day War was declared, the Gloves under the Armour, which you will remember hung on the left side of the Church, fell to the floor. Mr Hood made a lot of the coincidence imagining the spirit of the old Knight in the Gloves, and said he would restore the Gloves to their place on the day the War ended, but as you know he died last year. The present Vicar, however, carried out his wishes, and carefully refixed the Gloves, while the children watched. Then we sang the National Anthem and the children formed a long procession and marched up and down the street till it was time to go home.

After tea our Church Clock, which had been silent all through the War, struck at 6 and has continued striking day and night. It may seem a little thing to you, but to all here it meant much, and sounded like the voice of an old friend returning from the grave.

On Thursday evening we had a Thanksgiving Service in Church, and it would have done your heart good to see the crowd and to hear the good old hymns as they were sung. In all the services I have attended I never felt one like this, everyone was so excited and yet so thoroughly reverent and in earnest, that the very air seemed full of electricity, and so unlike the deadly dull services we all know, that there was a feeling of unreality about it all.

The War has pressed more heavily on us than is generally thought, even by ourselves, and I am afraid has aged us more than the 4½ years warrant as regards time, and this is especially true with those whose loved ones were fighting, positions of danger. The first thing on waking and the last thing at night, and often in the night when unable to sleep, one's thoughts naturally turned to those in peril and try as you would you could not help worrying. The coming of post was always tinged with dread of the news it might bring, and when no news was received the suspense of waiting was a sore trouble.

There was also a general War weariness which showed itself in people, reading news of great victories as though they were quite ordinary episodes in our everyday lives, besides which accounts of suffering or of horrible cruelty to helpless people failed to rouse the indignation of earlier days. It certainly appeared as though our feelings were blunted as regards those not directly connected with us, but specially sharpened as far as those near and dear to us were concerned.

I think most people feel that some time must elapse before we can properly celebrate peace, our feelings have been too much harrassed and our sympathies too often called for. As I look back over the last 4½ years I can see so many tragedies in families I know well, and I can see so many of my old boys who are dead and wounded, or dying of consumption, and recall them as boys at school where I used to urge on them the duty of patriotism, so that at present, it doesn't seem right that those who have escaped shall give themselves up to Joy days.

I have suggested to the Vicar that when our boys return we should have a special Reunion Service of Thanksgiving for those who have escaped death. He quite agrees and also wishes to have another Memorial Service for all those who have fallen. . . .

I am posting to you today the *Express* of Monday and the *Chronicle* of Tuesday, not so much for the contents as for the Historical interest that will attach to them in the future. Many people are carefully saving newspapers for future generations. Now to return to my old theme, 'Weather'.

Since Monday we have had clear, bright frosty weather with E. wind, our bedroom thermometer registered 45° this morning and Ma, sitting up in bed with multitudinous garments surmounted with an Army Blanket from her shoulders, shuddered to see me washing in cold water. As regards post we heard from Wally this morning, from Ron earlier in the week saying he had been given a new Airship, and a PC from Bob acknowledging some garments we sent. Em returned from Leyton last night, but she is tired out and is staying in bed today.

It's time I stopped as my pen keeps making mistakes.
Dad

Only three members of the Saunders family are alive today. Mrs Louise Downer, a widow and a former headmistress, lives on her own in a flat in Eastbourne. Ronald, who emigrated to Canada like his eldest brother William, is a retired chartered accountant living in Winnipeg with his Canadian wife. Bertram, also a retired chartered accountant, lives with his wife at Rotherfield in Sussex.

It was Mrs Downer (the 'middle one' of the family and the first to be born in Fletching) who brought her father's letters to the notice of the Imperial War Museum, when being interviewed about her experiences in the WAAC in France. At the age of eighty-eight her memories of the past are blurred but the letters bring vividly back to her the war years in Fletching.

'I take my hat off to my parents every time I look back to those days' she says. 'It's a marvel how they kept going with all they had to do at their age, and still found time for entertaining and regular letters to all of us away from home. They were often almost at the end of their tether, but I remember them as devoted to each other. The frictions my father mentions were written tongue-in-cheek – he had a great sense of humour. It was

209

because they were so different in temperament. Father was quieter, not so demonstrative. Mother was very outspoken, she hid nothing. I can see her now, looking every inch a duchess.'

Among the family photographs that people her flat, 'Ma' is instantly recognisable: ramrod-erect in an ankle-length gown, firm-lipped, with a direct look at the camera. More informally 'Pa' is pictured tending plants in his greenhouse, a lean-faced, handsome man with a white moustache, sporting a pipe and Panama hat. 'Bumble Bee and Butterfly', they settled in Sutton, Surrey, after retirement and lived in amicable contention until the Second World War.

In 1974 Lu and Bert attended the 150th anniversary of Fletching School, changed almost out of recognition from the school they had attended under the parental eye, when lessons were held in two large classrooms and the cane was not infrequently administered. Bert recalled an occasion when his father (known by the children as 'Master') was ill and his mother ('Governess') took his place. After announcing at Assembly that 'Master' would be returning the following Monday, his mother was sitting by an open window when she overheard a boy say to another: 'I'll be glad when Master's back, I'd rather a caning than Governess's blooming jaw.'

To the tourist Fletching is a picture village (rated the best-kept village in Sussex in 1977). To Mrs Downer it is a shell of the village she remembers from childhood. The well-to-do and retired inhabit its old houses. Mr Fenner's farm is owned by comedian Jimmy Edwards and managed by his elder brother Alan. The interior of the Griffin is more immaculately olde-worlde than ever it was in the days when farm-labourers and Tommies were its mainstay. From nearby Sheffield Park station a steam train still runs, but no longer to London. Preservationists acquired a five-mile stretch of the old line in 1959. They call it the Bluebell Line.

St Mary's House (still with its Latin inscription above the door, Res non Verba, Deeds not Words) has been converted into two separate dwellings. At the back there are lawns and flowerbeds where Pa tended his vegetables and fruit trees. And in the meadows and woods beyond he would find few of the wild flowers that had so often brightened his day.

There is no one now in the village who remembers the Saunders family and only a war memorial to recall those momentous years. A history of the church, on sale to tourists who come from many parts of the world, gives prominence to two names: Simon de Montfort, who came with his barons to pray here on the eve of the Battle of Lewes in 1264: and Edward Gibbon, who was buried in the Sheffield Mausoleum in 1794.

Few will make much of a passing comment in one paragraph in the history: 'In the nave are hung some accoutrements of the famous Nevill family, the Earls of Abergavenny, who were once the lords of the manor. Their date is about 1720, and they were restored in 1965 by the Master of Armouries of the Tower of London. They comprise a helmet, sword, gauntlets, spurs, etc., all in a good state of preservation. The gauntlets fell just before the start of the Crimean War and again before the Great War.'

Robert Saunders might have had something to say about the fact that no mention is made of the gauntlets having been ceremoniously restored to their place, on the afternoon of 11 November 1918.